CCPs provide long term guidance for management decisions and set forth goals, objectives, and strategies needed to accomplish refuge purposes and identify the Service's best estimate of future needs. These plans detail program planning levels that are sometimes substantially above current budget allocations and, as such, are primarily for Service strategic planning and program prioritization purposes. The plans do not constitute a commitment for staffing increases, operational and maintenance increases, or funding for future land acquisition.

Kern and Pixley National Wildlife Refuges

Comprehensive Conservation Plan

Prepared by:
U.S. Fish and Wildlife Service
Region 1

California/Nevada Refuge Planning Office
2800 Cottage Way, W-1916
Sacramento, CA 95825

Kern National Wildlife Refuge Complex
10811 Corcoran Road
Delano, CA 93215

Approved: _____   Date: _____
        California Nevada Operations Manager

Implementation of this Comprehensive Conservation Plan and alternative management actions/programs have been assessed consistent with the requirements of the National Environmental Policy Act (42 USC 4321 et seq.).

Table of Contents

Figures

Tables

Appendices

Chapter 1. Introduction

This document is a Comprehensive Conservation Plan (CCP) designed to guide management at Kern National Wildlife Refuge Complex (Refuge Complex) for the next 15 years. This Refuge Complex has two refuges, the Kern National Wildlife Refuge (Kern Refuge) and the Pixley National Wildlife Refuge (Pixley Refuge). The purposes of this CCP are:

- To provide a clear statement of direction for the future management of Kern and Pixley Refuges (Refuges);
- To provide long-term continuity in Refuge Complex management;
- To communicate the U.S. Fish and Wildlife Service's (Service) management priorities for the Refuges to their neighbors, visitors, and the general public;
- To provide an opportunity for the public to help shape the future management of the Refuges;
- To ensure that management programs on the Refuges are consistent with the mandates of the National Wildlife Refuge System (Refuge System) and the purposes for which the Refuges were established;
- To ensure that the management of the Refuges is consistent with Federal, State, and local plans; and
- To provide a basis for budget requests to support the Refuge's needs for staffing, operations, maintenance, and capital improvements.

This CCP describes the desired future conditions and provides long-range guidance to accomplish the purposes for which the Refuges were established. The CCP and environmental assessment (EA) address Service legal mandates, policies, goals, and National Environmental Policy Act (NEPA) compliance. A range of administrative, habitat management and visitor services alternatives that consider issues and opportunities on the Refuges are presented in the accompanying EA (Appendix A). The Service's initial proposal for future management of the Refuges is presented in this document. The final CCP will be developed through modifications made during the internal and public review processes.

Northern pintail. Dave Menke photo.

Major issues to be addressed during the CCP process include: habitat protection and enhancement; endangered species management; wetland restoration and management; nonnative vegetation control; visitor services management including hunting, wildlife observation, photography, interpretation and environmental education, and recreation; visitor services facilities; law enforcement; and visitor services compatibility.

As a management tool for the Refuge Complex staff to use, this CCP would guide management decisions, and describe strategies for achieving Refuge goals and objectives within its 15-year life. The CCP is divided into six chapters: Chapter 1, Introduction; Chapter 2, Planning Process; Chapter 3, Refuge and Resources Descriptions; Chapter 4, Problems and Opportunities; Chapter 5, Refuge Management Direction: Goals, Objectives and Strategies; and Chapter 6, Plan Implementation.

Refuge Overview

Introduction to Kern and Pixley Refuges

Kern and Pixley Refuges are part of a network of 15 national wildlife refuges and wildlife management areas in California's Central Valley and San Francisco Bay region that provide wintering habitat for migratory waterfowl and other waterbirds in the Pacific Flyway (Figure 1). The Refuges are located in the southern end of California's San Joaquin Valley (Figure 2). Chapter 4 presents a detailed description of the natural resources on Kern and Pixley Refuges.

Refuge Establishment and Acquisition History

Kern Refuge. When the area and number of wetlands and private duck clubs decreased during the 1930s and 1940s, Kern County sportsmen became alarmed. During this same time, the Service was actively pursuing suitable land for establishing wildlife refuges in Kern, Kings, and Tulare Counties. In 1957, the Service began negotiating with the Allison Honer Company for the purchase of 16 sections of land in northwest Kern County.

On March 11, 1958, the Migratory Bird Conservation Commission, under the authority of the Migratory Bird Conservation Act, approved the purchase of lands to create the Mariposa National Wildlife Refuge, known today as the Kern National Wildlife Refuge.

On November 18, 1960, the Service purchased 10,544 acres from the Allison Honer Company. On September 16, 1963, an additional 74 acres were purchased from Miller and Lux. to obtain the remaining acreage within the approved and current 10,618-acre Kern Refuge boundary (Figure 3).

Justification for establishing the Kern Refuge included:
■ Construction of Lake Isabella Reservoir reduced the areas available for waterfowl use in this ancestral wintering ground of the birds of the Pacific Flyway.

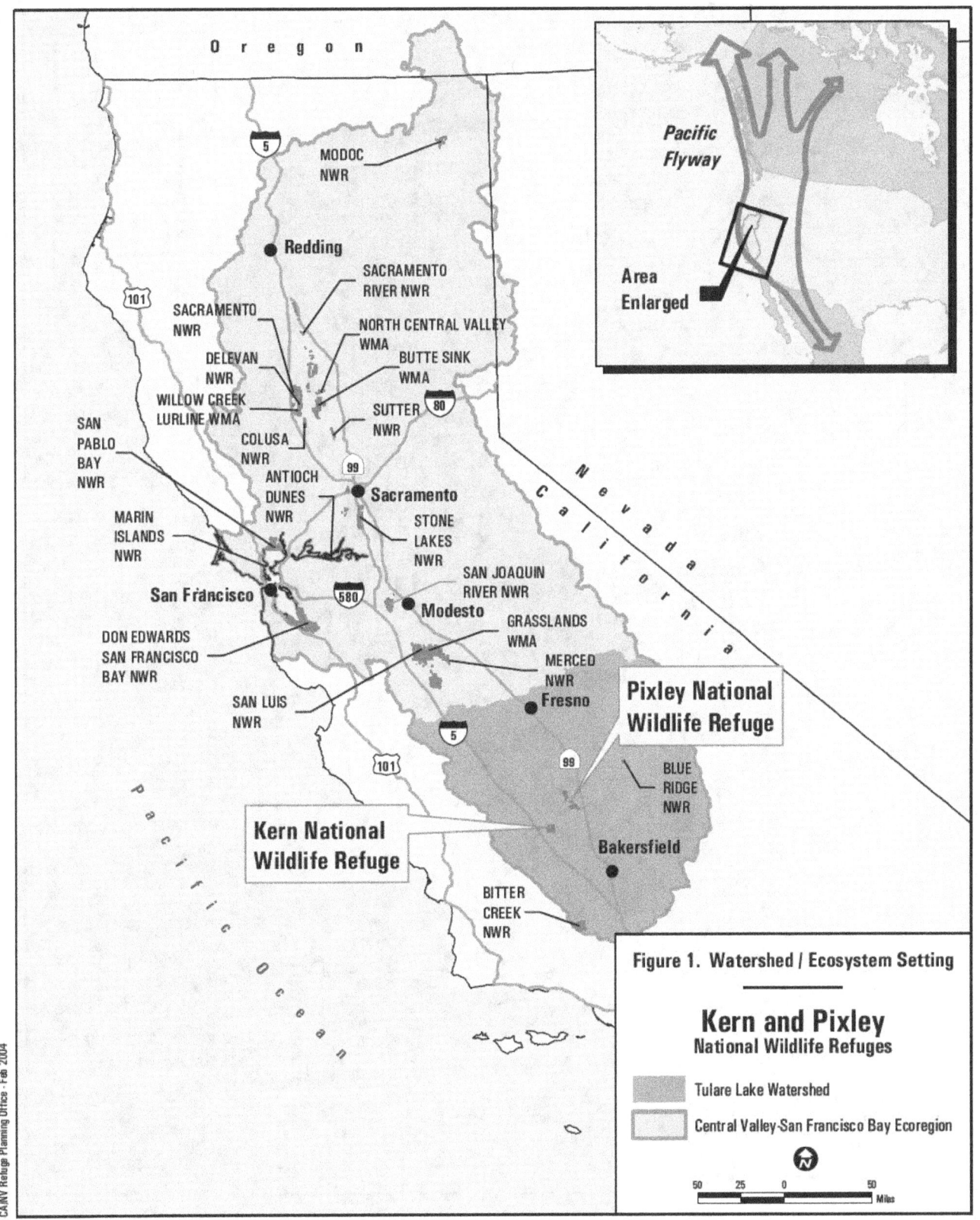

Figure 1. Watershed / Ecosystem Setting

Kern and Pixley
National Wildlife Refuges

Tulare Lake Watershed

Central Valley-San Francisco Bay Ecoregion

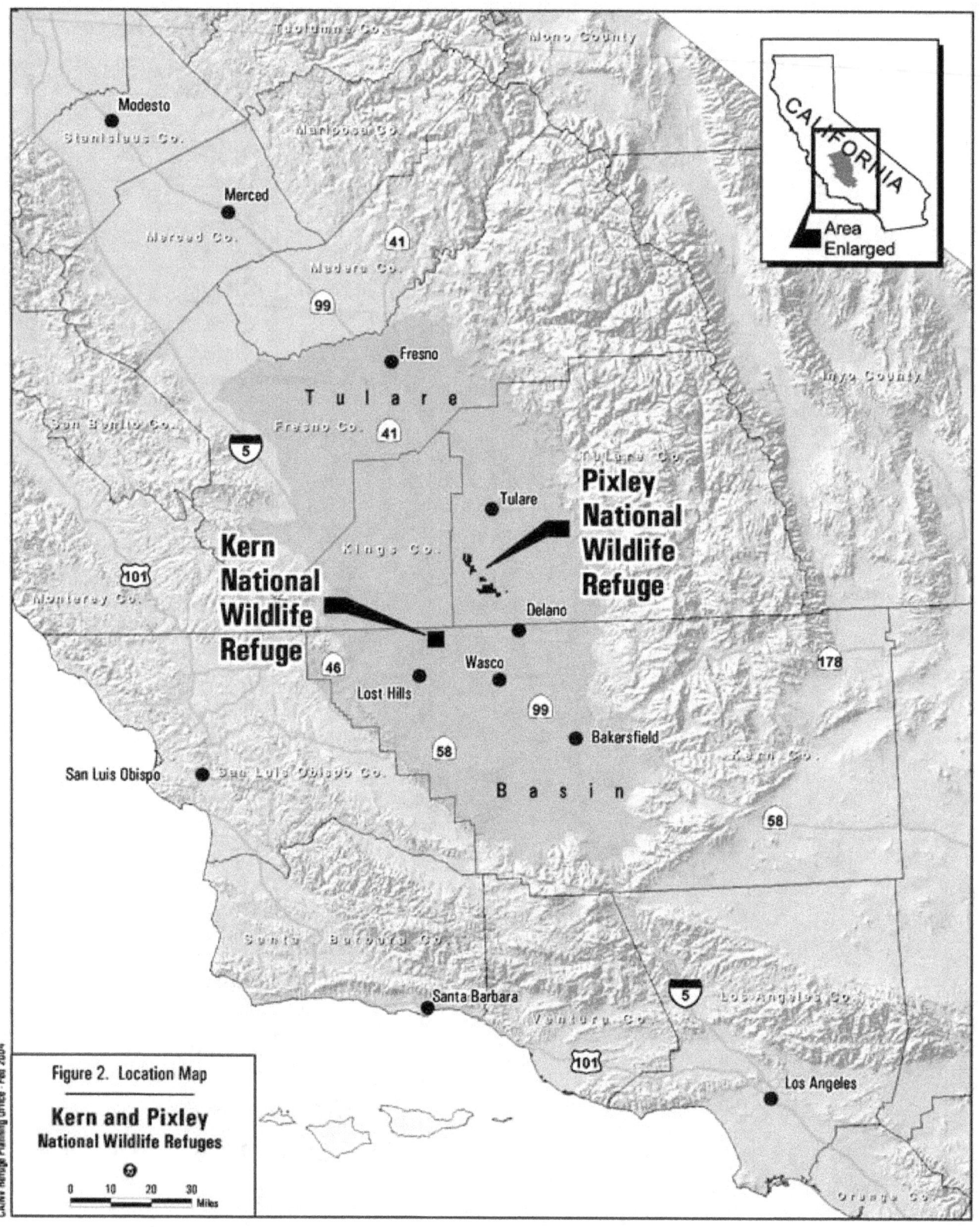

Figure 2. Location Map

Kern and Pixley
National Wildlife Refuges

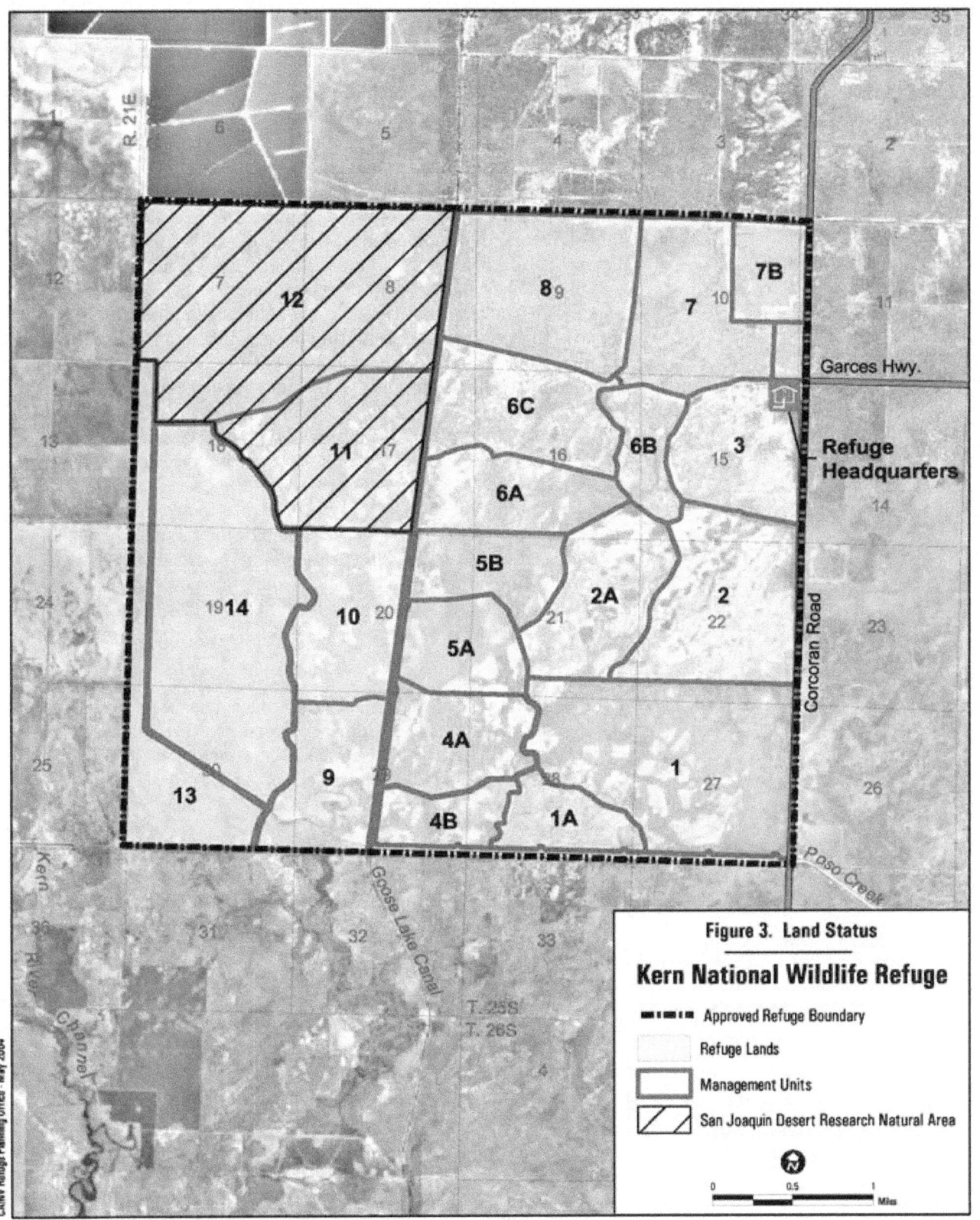

Figure 3. Land Status

Kern National Wildlife Refuge

- ▪▬▪▬▪ Approved Refuge Boundary
- Refuge Lands
- Management Units
- ⧄ San Joaquin Desert Research Natural Area

0   0.5   1
Miles

■ Agricultural and other development have reduced waterfowl wintering habitat (feeding and resting areas) until the lack of such habitat has become the principal limiting factor in the maintenance of the waterfowl resource in the Pacific Flyway. It is essential that additional habitat be provided for the maintenance of the resource.

■ The Kern site would obtain better distribution of the waterfowl throughout the wintering grounds, thereby alleviating the present trend toward increasingly heavy concentrations farther north.

■ Would provide opportunity for public hunting in the area.

■ Establishing and developing the refuge would replace part of the waterfowl habitat lost to agricultural and other development in a region formerly used heavily by migrating and wintering birds. Restoring this habitat would attract and hold large numbers of waterfowl, thereby improving hunting opportunities in the general area and, by obtaining wider distribution of the wintering population, reduce waterfowl depredations to crops in the lower San Joaquin Valley (MBCC 1958, Service 1961).

A number of entities hold easements on portions of Kern Refuge. Kern County was granted 30-foot wide easements on the east, west, and south boundaries for public roads. There are also two 10-foot wide gas pipeline easements, a 25-foot wide electric power line easement, and a 15,000 square-foot easement for a gas dehydration station. A perpetual water distribution easement on the Goose Lake Canal may now be terminated. The Service claims that a five-year period of non-use reverts control of the four-mile stretch to the Refuge. This claim has yet to be legally determined.

Pixley Refuge. In the 1920s and 1930s, title to large areas of former homestead tracks near Pixley, California reverted to the United States government. These lands, which were considered marginal for farming, were administered by the U.S. Department of Agriculture (USDA) under the Bankhead-Jones Farm Tenant Act.

On November 6, 1958, Executive Order 10787 transferred more than two million acres of USDA lands, including approximately 4,350 acres in Tulare County, to the U.S. Department of Interior. On November 17, 1959, the land in Tulare County was transferred to the Service under the Secretary of the Interior Order 2843. This action created Pixley Refuge, which was to be administered under the Migratory Bird Conservation Act for migratory birds and other wildlife.

From 1964 through 1966, the under the authority of the Migratory Bird Conservation Act, the Service exchanged approximately 607 acres of land at Pixley Refuge for approximately 410 acres of land. This action was done primarily to acquire inholdings within the Refuge boundary.

On January 7, 1980, under the authority of the Endangered Species Act of 1973, the Service Director approved an expanded boundary for Pixley Refuge. This action identified approximately 4,600 acres of land that could be acquired for the protection of the endangered blunt-nosed leopard lizard. The Refuge boundary was expanded again in the 1985

Master Plan. The current approved refuge boundary contains approximately 10,300 acres, of which the Service owns approximately 6,385 acres in fee; and 4.5 acres are under easement with a private landowner for access purposes (Figure 4). The remaining 3,911 acres are privately owned.

Many of the 27 parcels that the Service owns at Pixley Refuge have easements, rights-of-way, and outstanding mineral rights held by other entities. The most significant of these are the access easements to the Deer Creek Channel and County Road 88, which run through the Refuge.

Special Designations. In 1974, the San Joaquin Desert Research Natural Area (RNA) was established at Kern Refuge to preserve 2,260 acres of native upland. The RNA originally included all Refuge lands west of Goose Lake Canal in units 11 and 12 and the northern third of unit 14. In 1995, the northern third of unit 14 was removed from the RNA and unit 10 was added. In accordance with the Service's refuge planning policy, a wilderness review of Kern and Pixley Refuges was conducted during the CCP process (see Appendix B). Neither refuge was found suitable for wilderness designation.

Partnerships. Partnerships with various organizations and agencies have greatly expanded opportunities for both Kern and Pixley Refuges to achieve goals and objectives by implementing habitat improvement, biological monitoring, and public use projects. Both Ducks Unlimited and California Waterfowl Association have secured and implemented grants for habitat improvement projects on Kern Refuge that essentially doubled the quantity of moist soil habitat and significantly improved water management capabilities throughout the Refuge. Agreements with the Endangered Species Recovery Program operating from California State University Stanislaus permit their biologists to monitor refuge populations of endangered species, greatly supplementing the data gathering efforts of Refuge staff.

Tulare County Audubon (TCA) obtained a matching fund grant from the National Fish and Wildlife Foundation to construct a self-guided interpretive trail on Pixley Refuge. The Service then funded an observation platform that was constructed at the terminus of the trail primarily with volunteer labor provided by TCA members. This was the first time that any portion of Pixley Refuge has been open to unsupervised use by the public.

The longest standing cooperative association for the Refuge Complex is with the California Department of Fish and Game (CDFG). Operating continuously since 1973 through this agreement, the public hunting program on Kern Refuge is administered by the CDFG. In addition to the hunt program, CDFG also works cooperatively with the Service to monitor and when necessary, manage waterfowl disease outbreaks in the southern San Joaquin Valley.

Without the cooperative efforts of these and other organizations and agencies, the scope and depth of Refuge programs would be significantly reduced.

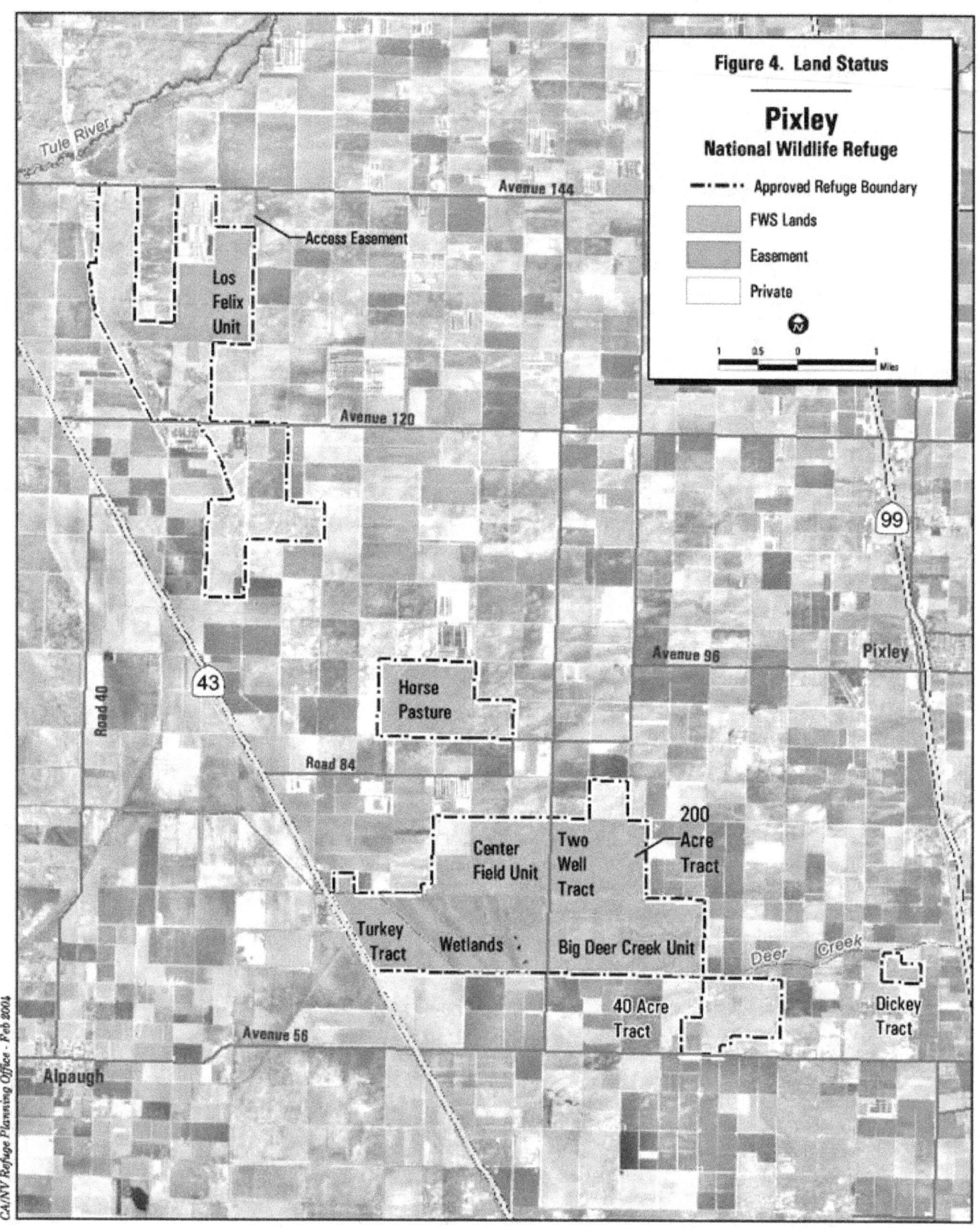

Figure 4. Land Status

Pixley
National Wildlife Refuge

–··–··– Approved Refuge Boundary

FWS Lands

Easement

Private

Tule River

Avenue 144

Access Easement

Los Felix Unit

Avenue 120

99

Road 40

43

Avenue 96

Pixley

Horse Pasture

Road 84

200 Acre Tract

Center Field Unit

Two Well Tract

Turkey Tract

Wetlands

Big Deer Creek Unit

Deer Creek

Dickey Tract

40 Acre Tract

Avenue 56

Alpaugh

CA/NV Refuge Planning Office - Feb 2004

Management History
Kern Refuge
Prior to establishment of Kern Refuge, much of the land that is now part of units 13 and 14 were actively farmed by the Allison Horner Company for a variety of small grain crops. To allow for cultivation of these fields, much of the area was partially leveled and numerous levees and canals were constructed throughout the area to facilitate water distribution and drainage. Approximately 1,400 acres west of Goose Lake Canal were manipulated in this way.

Historic management of the area east of Goose Lake Canal consisted primarily of grazing by both cattle and sheep. While this area did not consistently contain wetlands, the area was characterized by uplands that supported perennial grasses and scrub vegetation interspersed with swales that contained water during years of normal or higher precipitation.

Early development of the Refuge focused primarily on the area east of Goose Lake Canal with an emphasis on creating wetlands. This included drilling 10 deep water wells, construction or renovation of 35 miles of levees, excavation of 7 miles of water distribution ditches, and placement of numerous water control structures. Additionally, an extensive system of levee supported roads was developed and used for water management, public access, and all weather access to critical areas of the Refuge.

While much of the developed area consisted of seasonal marsh, approximately 1,200 acres within units 4, 5, and 6 were leveled to allow maximum use of the limited water supplies available to the Refuge, and managed as moist soil units.

During the initial development of the Refuge, water to support the newly developed wetlands was to be supplied from wells drilled on the east half of the Refuge. When this source became cost prohibitive and the well output was insufficient to meet Refuge needs, the purchase of surface water was pursued. Due to Refuge budget constraints, water sufficient to flood only approximately 2,500 acres, was normally available. The passage of the Central Valley Project Improvement Act in 1992 provided the Refuge with a more reliable and abundant water supply. Now that full development (Level 4) water supplies are being obtained by the Bureau of Reclamation, approximately 6,400 acres of wetlands can be flooded and maintained on the Refuge. For a more detailed description of water development and management on Kern Refuge see the Water section in Chapter 3 (page 26).

This dramatic increase in water availability has changed the overall management and appearance of the Refuge. The Service now manages a greater quantity and variety of wetland habitats on the Refuge including: summer water for colonial nesting species such as great blue herons and white-faced ibis; late summer waterfowl habitat for early migrant ducks; greatly expanded opportunities to provide moist soil habitat; and greater flexibility in irrigation schedules of marsh vegetation.

Pixley Refuge

Historic records indicate that the western portion of the Pixley Refuge had been extensively cultivated while the eastern areas were used primarily as grazing land. For some undocumented reason, possibly increased soil salinity, farming on the lands that eventually became the Refuge was abandoned. At the time of Refuge establishment, no farming was being conducted. Areas in the Center Field Unit still show evidence of cultivation and the existence of irrigation or drainage ditches and small reservoirs.

Blunt-nosed leopard lizard. Fish & Wildlife Service photo.

Beginning in 1963 and continuing into the following year, initial development of the Refuge included the creation of a series of wetland impoundments in Sections 19, 20 and 21 that totaled 797 acres. In an effort to supply the water needs of the Refuge, an irrigation well was drilled in 1962 but failed to produce the necessary quantity of water. With inadequate wells, water supplies for the Refuge were limited to seasonal runoff from the Deer Creek watershed and were only available in years of high precipitation and normally occurred late in the winter or early spring. Due to this sporadic nature of the wetlands on the Refuge, only limited use of the area by waterfowl occurred until development of a high production water well in 1992.

With the advent of a reliable well, active management of approximately one-half of the wetlands began in earnest when a moist soil management program was initiated in 1992. The response by waterfowl and waterbirds to the availability of wetlands in the Tulare Lake basin was excellent.

During the initial acquisition of lands for the Pixley Refuge, approximately 3,180 acres of uplands were acquired. With passage of the Endangered Species Act in 1973, management of these uplands for the benefit of listed species, took on additional importance. Between 1981 and 1994, an additional 2,230 acres of uplands were acquired for the management of threatened and endangered species.

In an effort to improve the annual grasslands on the Refuge for the benefit of the listed species present, a closely monitored grazing program utilizing cattle supplied by Refuge permittees was initiated. To facilitate this program, a stock water well was drilled in the Center Field Unit in 1972. This is the only active program currently in place to effectively manage the uplands of the Refuge.

National Wildlife Refuge System Mission and Goals

Established in 1903 by President Theodore Roosevelt, the 94-million-acre Refuge System now includes over 540 National Wildlife Refuges, thousands of small wetlands, and other special management areas in 50 states and several territories. Most National Wildlife Refuges are strategically located along the major bird migration corridors, ensuring that ducks, geese, and songbirds have rest stops on their annual migrations. Many refuges were established to protect endangered or threatened species or key sensitive habitats, such as offshore nesting seabird colonies.

The mission of the Refuge System is to administer a national network of lands and waters for the conservation, management, and where appropriate, restoration of the fish, wildlife, and plant resources and their habitats within the United States for the benefit of present and future generations of Americans (National Wildlife Refuge System Improvement Act of 1997).

The goals of the Refuge System are:
- To preserve, restore, and enhance in their natural ecosystems (when practicable) all species of animals and plants that are endangered or threatened with becoming endangered;
- To perpetuate the migratory bird resource;
- To preserve a natural diversity and abundance of fauna and flora on refuge lands;
- To provide an understanding and appreciation of fish and wildlife ecology and the human's role in the environment; and
- To provide refuge visitors with high-quality, safe, wholesome, and enjoyable wildlife-oriented recreational experiences, to the extent that these activities are compatible with the purposes for which the refuge was established.

Other Landscape-Level Goals

Several different landscape-level plans and programs have goals that are applicable to Kern and Pixley Refuges, including:
- CALFED Ecosystem Restoration Program;
- Central Valley Habitat Joint Venture Implementation Plan;
- Riparian Bird Conservation Plan (California Partners in Flight and the Riparian Habitat Joint Venture);
- Pacific Flyway Management Plan: Western Management Unit Mourning Dove;
- Southern Pacific Coast Regional Shorebird Plan;
- Kern County General Plan;
- Recovery Plan for Upland Species of the San Joaquin Valley, California; and

Refuge System Mission:
". . . to administer a national network of lands and waters for the conservation, management, and where appropriate, restoration of the fish, wildlife, and plant resources and their habitats within the United States for the benefit of present and future generations of Americans"

- Service/California Department of Fish and Game Tricolored Blackbird Status Update and Management Guidelines.

The relevant goals from each of these plans are listed in Appendix C.

Refuge Purposes

The Service acquires Refuge System lands under a variety of legislative acts and administrative orders. The transfer and acquisition authorities, used to obtain the lands, usually have one or more purposes for which land can be transferred or acquired. These purposes, along with the Refuge System mission, form the basis from which and the standard by which the Service determines if refuge uses are compatible.

Kern Refuge was established under the authority of the Migratory Bird Conservation Act for use ". . . as an inviolate sanctuary, or for any other management purpose, for migratory birds" (16 U.S.C. § 715d).

Pixley Refuge was established to provide wintering habitat for migratory birds and protect habitat for the endangered blunt-nosed leopard lizard. The authorities and corresponding purposes for which Pixley Refuge was established are: (1) Bankhead-Jones Farm Tenant Act ". . . a land-conservation and land-utilization program . . ." 7 U.S.C. § 1011; (2) Secretarial Order 2843, dated Nov. 17, 1959 ". . . for migratory birds and other wildlife . . ."; and (3) Endangered Species Act of 1973 ". . . to conserve (A) fish or wildlife which are listed as endangered species or threatened species . . . or (B) plants . . ." 16 U.S.C. § 1534.

Refuge Vision Statements

A vision statement is a concise statement of what a refuge should be, based primarily on the Refuge System mission, specific refuge purposes, and other mandates. A vision statement helps articulate the direction the refuge should be heading. Vision statements for Kern and Pixley Refuges follow:

Kern Refuge

Kern Refuge is representative of a once extensive complex of native wetlands and uplands and currently is the largest wetland complex managed for wildlife in the southern San Joaquin Valley. With a secure water supply, Kern Refuge will provide reliable, high-quality wetland habitat to meet the needs of wintering and migrating waterfowl and waterbirds. The Refuge's riparian corridors and seasonal wetlands will support a rich diversity of migratory songbirds, colonial nesting species, and raptors. Remnant valley-floor uplands will be preserved and restored for native plant and animal species. These uplands will support populations of threatened and endangered species including the blunt-nosed leopard lizard, Tipton kangaroo rat, San Joaquin kit fox, and Buena Vista Lake shrew. To meet the demands of the rapidly growing population of the southern San Joaquin Valley and to accommodate more than 50,000 visitors annually, the Refuge will provide opportunities for high-quality wildlife-dependent visitor services, including hunting, wildlife observation, environmental education, and interpretation. These visitor services opportunities will increase the public's understanding of and appreciation for wildlife and the importance of conserving their habitat.

Pixley Refuge

Pixley Refuge represents one of the few remaining examples of the grasslands, vernal pools, and playas that once bordered the historic Tulare Lake. Management of these diverse natural communities will focus on providing high-quality habitat for threatened and endangered species including the blunt-nosed leopard lizard, Tipton kangaroo rat, San Joaquin kit fox, and vernal pool fairy shrimp. Natural lands between the Refuges will be protected through conservation easements, partnerships, and willing-seller acquisition to provide linkage areas for these species. Managed wetlands and adjacent grasslands will provide high-quality habitat for wintering and migratory waterfowl and waterbirds, including sandhill cranes. Restored riparian corridors will support a rich diversity of migratory songbirds and raptors. Pixley Refuge will provide unique opportunities for compatible wildlife-dependent visitor services which will increase the public's understanding of and appreciation for wildlife and the importance of conserving wildlife habitat.

Legal and Policy Guidance

Refuges are guided by the mission, goals, and purpose of the Refuge System, Service policy, legal mandates, international treaties, and refuge purposes. Key concepts in the laws, regulations, and policies that guide management of the Refuge System include primary versus multiple-use public lands, compatibility, and priority wildlife-dependent recreational activities. Examples of relevant guidance include the National Wildlife Refuge System Administration Act of 1966, as amended by the National Wildlife Refuge System Improvement Act of 1997 (Improvement Act), Refuge Recreation Act of 1962, Executive Order 12996 (Management and General Public Use of the National Wildlife Refuge System), and selected portions of the Code of Federal Regulations and the Service Manual.

The Refuge Recreation Act, as amended, authorized the Secretary of the Interior to administer refuges, hatcheries, and other conservation areas for recreational use when such uses did not interfere with the area's primary purpose. The National Wildlife Refuge System Administration Act of 1966, as amended, provides guidelines and directives for the administration and management of all areas in the Refuge System, for the protection and conservation of fish and wildlife threatened with extinction, wildlife ranges, game ranges, wildlife management areas, and waterfowl production areas. Use of any area within the Refuge System was permitted, provided that such uses were compatible with the major purposes for which such areas were established.

Executive Order 12996 (March 23, 1996) identified a new mission statement for the Refuge System; established six priority public uses (hunting, fishing, wildlife observation and photography, environmental education and interpretation); emphasized conservation and enhancement of the quality and diversity of fish and wildlife habitat; stressed the importance of partnerships with Federal and state agencies, tribes, organizations, industry, and the general public; mandated public involvement in decisions on the acquisition and management of refuges; and required identification, prior to acquisition of new refuge lands, of existing compatible wildlife-dependent uses that would be permitted to continue on an interim basis pending completion of comprehensive planning.

The Improvement Act defined a unifying mission for the Refuge System; established the legitimacy and appropriateness of the six priority visitor services; established a formal process for determining compatibility; established the responsibilities of the Secretary of the Interior for managing and protecting the Refuge System; and required a CCP for each refuge by the year 2012. The Improvement Act amended portions of the Refuge Recreation Act and National Wildlife Refuge System Administration Act of 1966.

Unlike other Federal lands, which are managed under a multiple-use mandate (e.g., national forests administered by the Forest Service and public lands administered by the Bureau of Land Management), the Refuge System is managed specifically for the benefit of fish, wildlife, and plant resources and their habitats. Compatible wildlife-dependent recreation is a legitimate and appropriate general visitor service of the Refuge System. Wildlife-dependent public uses include hunting, fishing, wildlife observation and photography, and environmental education and interpretation are priority visitor services of the Refuge System. These uses must receive enhanced consideration over other visitor services in refuge planning and management.

Before any uses, including wildlife-dependent recreational activities, are allowed on a refuge, Federal law requires that they be formally determined to be "compatible." A compatible use is defined as a use that, in the sound professional judgment of the refuge manager, would not materially interfere with or detract from the fulfillment of the Refuge System mission or the refuge purposes. Sound professional judgment is defined as a finding, determination, or decision that is consistent with: the principles of sound fish and wildlife management and administration, available science and resources (funding, personnel, facilities, and other infrastructure), and applicable laws. If financial resources were not available to design, operate, and maintain an activity, the refuge manager would take reasonable steps to obtain assistance from the state and other conservation interests.

The Service has completed draft compatibility determinations for the Refuges (Appendix D). Five of the six priority wildlife-dependent recreational activities were determined to be compatible for the Kern Refuge: hunting, wildlife observation, wildlife photography, environmental interpretation, and environmental education. Four of the six priority wildlife-dependent recreational activities were determined to be compatible for Pixley Refuge: wildlife observation, wildlife photography, environmental interpretation, and environmental education. Fishing was not evaluated at either Refuge due to the lack of fishing opportunities. Hunting was not evaluated at Pixley for two primary reasons. First, the Refuge's wetland unit is too small to manage as a hunt area. It would require a disproportionate amount of staff time and resources for the small number of hunters potentially accommodated. Second, Pixley Refuge is an important wintering area for sandhill cranes. The cranes are sensitive to disturbance and would likely stop using the Refuge if hunting were allowed.

Chapter 2. Planning Process

Planning Process, Planning Time Frame, and Future Revision

The first Planning Update for the Kern and Pixley Refuges CCP was distributed in August 1999. It announced public workshops held on August 30 and 31, 1999, to identify issues and concerns and described interim goals. In a Federal Register Notice dated August 16, 1999, the Service announced that it was preparing a CCP for Kern and Pixley Refuges. The second Planning Update, released in March 2000, described the issues, concerns, and opportunities identified at the public workshops, and the draft vision statements for the Refuges. The third Planning Update, released in March 2002, described the draft alternatives for managing Kern and Pixley Refuges.

The development of this draft CCP was guided by the Refuge Planning Chapter of the Fish and Wildlife Service Manual (Part 602 FW2.1, November 1996). Key steps included: (1) preplanning; (2) identifying issues and developing a vision; (3) gathering information; (4) analyzing resource relationships; (5) developing alternatives and assessing environmental effects (see Appendix F for environmental assessment); (6) identifying a preferred alternative; and (7) publishing the draft CCP. The next steps in this process include soliciting public comments on the draft CCP, preparing the final CCP, obtaining approval from the California/Nevada Operations Manager, and finally, implementing the CCP.

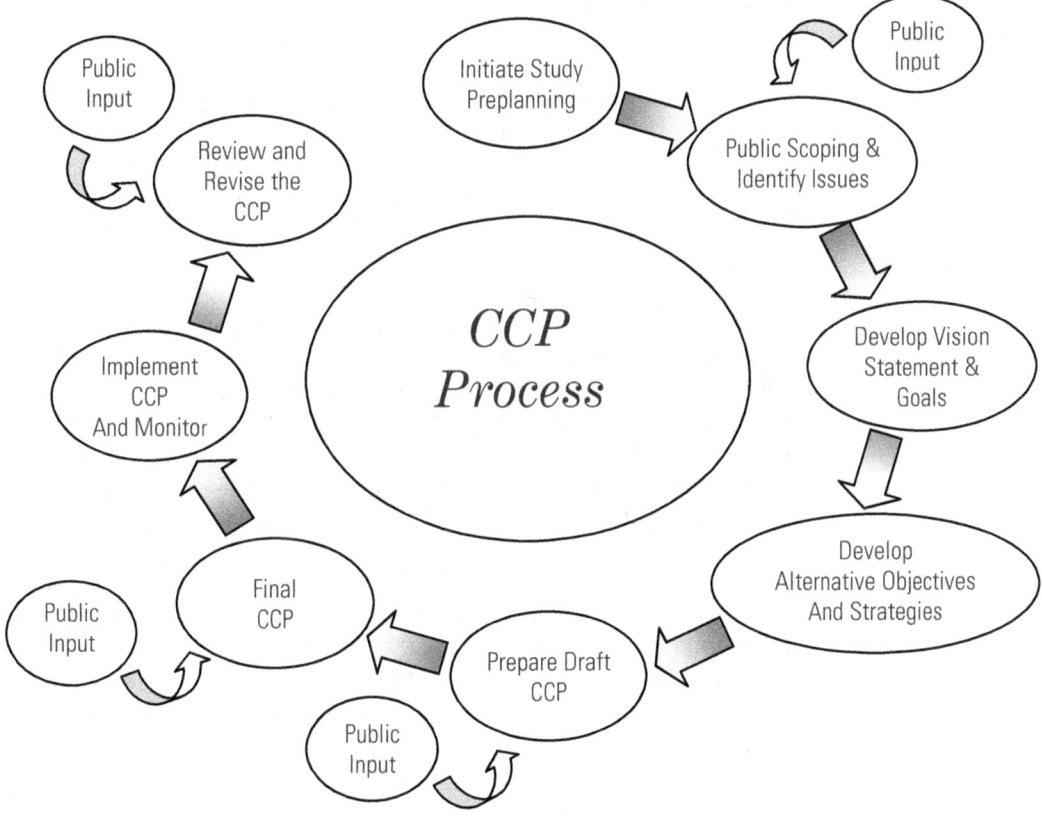

Figure 5. CCP Process.

Once finalized, this CCP will be annually reviewed by Refuge Complex staff while preparing work plans and updating the Refuge information management system database. It may also be reviewed during routine inspections or programmatic evaluations. Results of the reviews may indicate a need to modify the CCP. Monitoring objectives is an integral part of the CCP, and management activities may be modified if desired results are not achieved. If minor changes are required, the level of public involvement and associated NEPA documentation will be determined by the project leader. The CCP will be formally revised at least every 15 years.

Planning Issues

Issues, concerns, and opportunities were identified through discussions with planning team members, key contacts, and through the public scoping process, which began with two public workshops in August 1999. Verbal and written comments were received at the meetings. The following issues, concerns, and opportunities are a compilation of information developed by the Service throughout the planning process.

General

In general, commenters supported the Refuges and approved of the current management. Three people recommended that the CCP be coordinated with other conservation efforts in the region. One commenter suggested that Kern Refuge should be kept in its current condition. Another commenter stated that current water allocations should be maintained or increased if possible.

Wildlife and Habitat Management

The Service received a variety of comments relating to wildlife management. A few people commented on managing for specific species. For example, one commenter suggested that the Service replace chain link fencing with larger mesh to avoid a possible choking hazard to kit foxes. Another person suggested that Kern Refuge should emphasize management of tricolored blackbirds.

Several people commented on existing management practices at the Refuges. Three commenters suggested that cattle grazing should be continued as a management tool on the Refuges. Four people suggested that vegetation in unit 1 should be better controlled to provide more open water habitat. Another person commented that the Refuges should ensure that vegetation management practices in the marsh are sensitive to migratory birds that use vegetation in the spring and summer.

Other commenters suggested that the Service could adopt new wildlife management measures, including reintroducing large native game, or offering incentives to adjacent landowners to grow wildlife-friendly crops. Finally, one person suggested that the status and distribution information for all the natural resources on the Refuges should be updated.

Visitor services

The Service received more comments on visitor services than any other category. These comments fall into three main categories: facilities and staffing; hunting; and nonconsumptive recreation. Under the first category (facilities and staffing), commenters suggested building more public restrooms at Kern Refuge, with Service staff on the Refuge at all times to prevent vandalism. Other commenters suggested that more parking lots be made available at Kern Refuge and that a parking lot should be constructed for visitors to Pixley Refuge.

Comments on hunting were varied. Several commenters expressed support for the hunting program at Kern Refuge. Another commenter stated that hunting and trapping are not compatible with the Refuge purposes. Two people requested that more youth-hunt days be planned.

Several people commented on the areas open to hunting at Kern Refuge. Comments ranged from increasing the hunting area at Kern Refuge to closing particular units. Other commenters suggested rotating the open and closed units. One person requested that Pixley Refuge be opened to hunting.

Several people commented on the reservation system. Some comments supported the existing system while others were opposed to it and suggested changes. One person suggested that the Kern Refuge offer three types of hunting passes: hunting from blinds, free roaming, and hunting from dikes. Four commenters requested that more hunters be accommodated on hunt days.

A number of people suggested changes in the hunting regulations. Two commenters requested that the Service allow hunting on Sundays. One person suggested that hunters be allowed to start a half-hour or an hour earlier. Another person requested that the current 25-shell limit be maintained and that enforcement be increased. One commenter suggested that motion decoys be prohibited. Another person recommended that the Service adopt a blind limit of two adult hunters per blind.

The Service received a variety of comments and ideas on nonconsumptive recreation. One person suggested that a birder's board be established outside the new Refuge Complex office where birders could record their sightings. Two commenters suggested that the Service establish a second tour route at Kern Refuge that could be used by non-hunters on hunt days. Several comments addressed Pixley Refuge specifically. One commenter requested that a signed nature trail and viewing platform be developed at Pixley Refuge. Another person said the Service should address the liability issues of concurrent use by the public of areas where permittee livestock may interact with visitor services, such as birdwatching.

Outreach/Environmental Education

One commenter suggested that the Service produce an educational video about the Refuges and make a concerted effort to involve area schools. The same commenter suggested that the Service conduct a publicity campaign highlighting Refuge Complex restoration efforts and the resulting benefits. Finally, another person suggested that the Service put a Watchable Wildlife sign on Highway 99 to direct visitors to Pixley Refuge.

Acquisition

A number of commenters suggested that the Service expand the Refuges, to provide protected corridors between the Refuges and other conservation areas in the San Joaquin Valley. Another person suggested that the Service acquire lands at the boundaries of Kern Refuge to secure feeding habitat for tricolored blackbirds. Finally, another commenter recommended that the Service acquire the remaining private lands within the Pixley Refuge approved boundary.

Chapter 3. Refuge and Resource Descriptions

Geographic and Ecological Setting

Geographic Setting

The Refuge Complex is in the southern San Joaquin Valley (Valley) which is formed by the Sierra Nevada Mountains on the east and the Coastal Range on the west. Elevations in the Valley decrease toward the north and average 220 feet above mean sea level on the Refuge Complex. Historic and present drainage of the Valley and the Kern Complex is also toward the north.

Kern Refuge, surrounded by agricultural lands and private duck clubs, represents the largest area (10,600 acres) managed for wildlife and plants in the southern portion of the Valley. Two major highways, Interstate 5 and Highway 99, run north and south through the Valley and are 20 miles to the east and 10 miles to the west of the Kern Refuge, respectively. One public road, Corcoran Road, borders the entire eastern edge of Kern Refuge. The closest town, Delano, is 20 miles to the east with a population of 22,800. Bakersfield is about 40 miles to the southeast and Fresno is 70 miles north of the Refuge.

Pixley Refuge is surrounded by agricultural lands that support a growing dairy industry. Highway 99 is 9 miles to the east and Highway 43 is 3 miles to the west; both run north and south and are connected by Avenue 56, which is approximately 2 miles south of the Pixley Refuge. The closest towns are Alpaugh, 8 miles to the west with a population of 900, and Earlimart, 8 miles to the east with a population of 900. The Tulare, Visalia, and Hanford area, with a combined population of 138,000, is approximately 30 miles north of Pixley Refuge on State Highway 99.

Historic Environment

Geologic data and historic accounts describe the southern Valley as a vast sea that as recently as 100 years ago covered at least 800 square miles in Tulare, Kings, and Kern Counties (Howard 1979, PG&E 1970). Rivers and streams flowed from the Sierra Nevada Mountains to the east of the Valley creating lush wetlands, riparian corridors, and lake basins. Tulare Lake, the largest lake basin and lowest point in the Valley, served as an endpoint for this system. Outflow to the Pacific Ocean via the Sacramento-San Joaquin Delta to the north, occurred in flood years (Figure 6). Despite being the driest portion of the Central Valley, the Tulare Basin historically contained the largest block of wetland habitat in California (about 260,000 acres of permanent wetlands and another 260,000 acres of seasonal wetlands) (CVHJV 1990).

American settlement of the Tulare Lake Basin was spurred by development elsewhere in California, especially the increasing demand for food during the gold rush and the urbanization of San Francisco and the Sacramento-San Joaquin Delta (Preston 1981). By the 1860s, the once isolated and self-sufficient Tulare Lake Basin provided agricultural

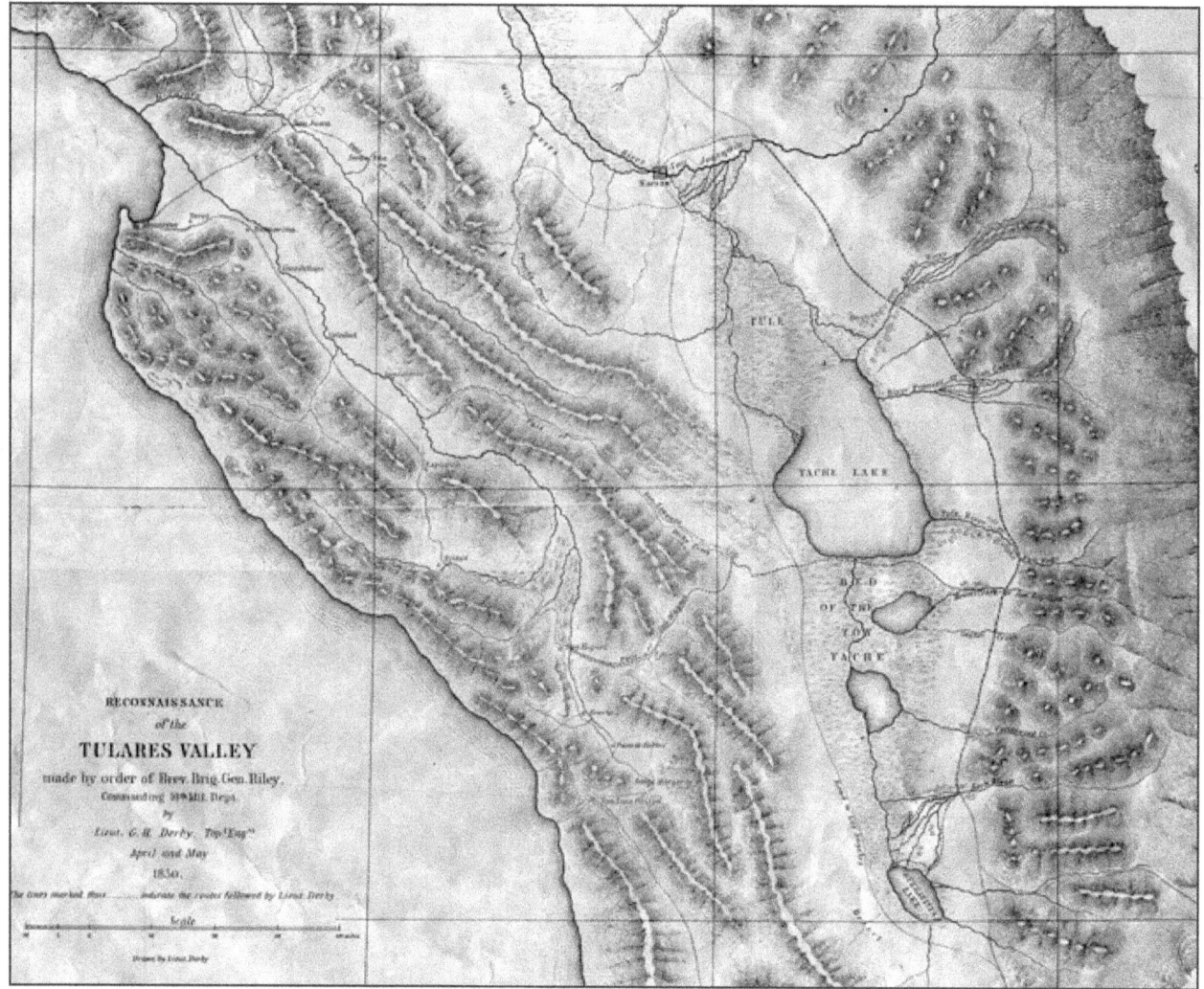

Figure 6. Map of the southern San Joaquin Valley by Lieutenant G. H. Derby, 1850. Note: Tulare Lake is labeled Tache Lake on this map.

crops to more urbanized areas in the State and was dependent on these areas for goods and services.

Agriculture played the most significant role in transforming the southern Valley from one dependent on natural processes, rainfall, and snowmelt, to one dependent on water diversions and groundwater pumping for the production of crops. While this greatly benefited the small agricultural communities that formed throughout the Valley, as more and more native uplands, wetlands, rivers and streams were converted to agricultural production, there were adverse impacts to native wildlife (Preston 1981). The extent of Tulare Lake and the supporting marshlands, smaller lake basins to the south, and rivers and streams from the Sierra Nevada Mountains to the east, were radically altered. By 1900, increased salinity and reduced water flows into the

Valley resulted in the demise of fisheries throughout the region as well as a large commercial fishing enterprise on Tulare Lake (Preston 1981).

Today, the southern Valley is characterized by a patchwork of agricultural fields, orchards, and vineyards connected to, and dependent on, a network of water districts and water delivery canals (Figure 7). Native wetlands are virtually nonexistent because the water has been diverted for agricultural purposes. When flooding occurs, the historic lake basins, marshes, streams, and rivers, that were converted to agricultural lands, still carry the majority of the water through the Valley. However, sheet flooding across urban and upland areas is common. Riparian habitat was once common along streams and rivers in the Central Valley. Katibah (1984) estimates that 92 percent to 95 percent of the Central Valley's riparian habitat has been lost. Riparian habitat on the Kern Refuge represents four percent to five percent of the land area and less than one percent on the Pixley Refuge. Uplands are in noncontiguous blocks surrounded by agriculture. From 1976 to 1980, 70 percent of habitat used by the endangered blunt-nosed leopard lizard had been lost to urbanization and agriculture (CDFG 2001). Other endangered species dependent on upland habitat such as the San Joaquin kit fox and Tipton kangaroo rat, have suffered similar losses. Range contraction, lack of upland habitat corridors, and competition with introduced species continue to adversely affect these animals.

Today, the Refuges represent some of the largest blocks of contiguous uplands (Pixley Refuge) and managed wetlands (Kern Refuge) in the southern Valley. Resident, migratory, and threatened and endangered species as well as native plants continue to use these lands throughout the year. While some of these species are found on and use private property, their last stronghold in the southern Valley may be the Refuges.

Soils
Kern Refuge
The five general soil types that have been mapped on the Kern Refuge include: Nahrub, partially drained-lethent complex (3,540 acres); Nahrub, drained-lethent complex (2,760 acres); Nahrub clay, drained (1,830 acres); Nahrub clay, partially drained (1,510 acres); and Garces silt loam (60 acres). When these soil types were mapped in 1982, 870 acres of the Refuge were flooded, and therefore not mapped. The Nahrub and Lethent soils formed in alluvium from primarily granitic and sedimentary rock. Nahrub soils occur as deep deposits (depths to 61 inches), with little to no surface slope, and poor drainage. They are composed of an upper layer of clay (0 to 34 inches) overlaying a lower layer of sandy loam, clay loam, and fine sandy loam. Lethent soils are also deep but are moderately well drained and are composed of a surface layer of silt loam (0 to 6 inches) over a clay layer up to 36 inches thick supported by loam to depths greater than 60 inches. Nahrub and Lethent soils are moderately to strongly saline-alkaline and may have

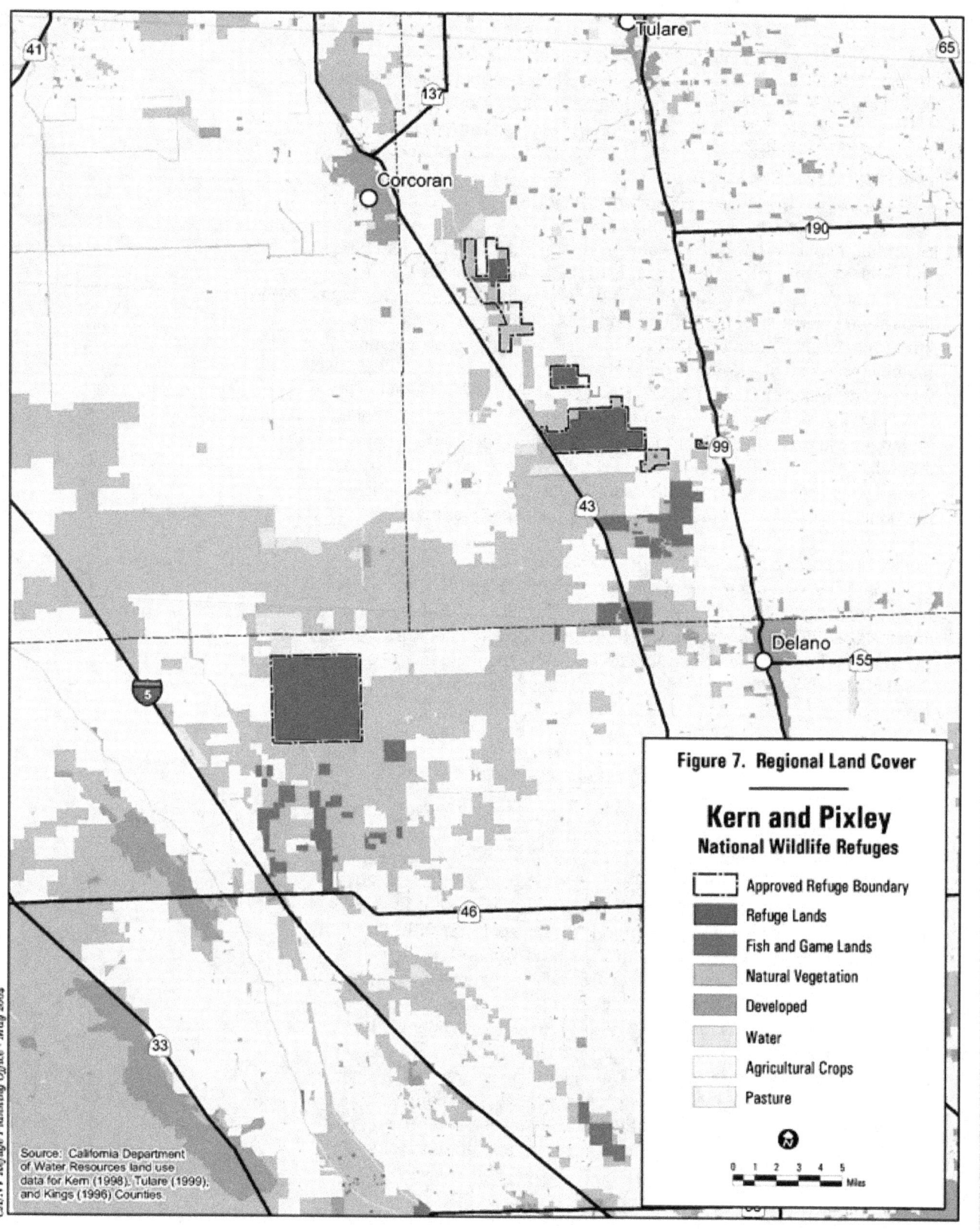

Figure 7. Regional Land Cover

Kern and Pixley
National Wildlife Refuges

- Approved Refuge Boundary
- Refuge Lands
- Fish and Game Lands
- Natural Vegetation
- Developed
- Water
- Agricultural Crops
- Pasture

Source: California Department of Water Resources land use data for Kern (1998), Tulare (1999), and Kings (1996) Counties.

CA/NV Refuge Planning Office - May 2004

toxic levels of boron present in some areas. Permeability is very slow and water capacity is low. A seasonally high water table limits rooting depth to three to six feet in Nahrub soils; however, rooting depths in Lethent soils are greater than five feet.

Garces silt loam is a deep (60 inches and greater) well-drained soil with little to no slope formed in alluvium derived from granitic rock. This soil is moderately to strongly saline-alkaline and may have toxic levels of boron present in some areas. While permeability is slow, rooting depths of greater than five feet are common.

Suitability of the Nahrub-Lethent and Garces soils for farming and grazing is poor to marginal. Farming is limited by slow to very slow permeability, clay textures, perched water table, and saline-alkaline conditions. These conditions, as well as annual rainfall, limit grazing. Only the Nahrub clay, partially drained and Garces soils are identified as soil types capable of supporting grazing within local rainfall and saline-alkaline constraints.

The characteristics and constraints of the soil types found on Kern Refuge indicate that new roads, levees and wetland units should not be developed from local soils. Periodic maintenance on roads and levees that support the auto tour route and regular Kern Refuge operations, incorporate suitable base material and surface aggregate from off-site. Less used interior roads and levees developed from on-site materials are occasionally impassable, especially during the wet winter months.

The soil types on the Kern Refuge have little effect on wetland management. Some shallower moist soil units are periodically farmed or subject to regular maintenance (disc, mow, burn, etc.) to manage wetland vegetation growth. Larger and deeper seasonal wetlands are not farmed but selected areas of vegetation are periodically managed to maintain and enhance open water habitat. During draw down and dry out of wetlands, the characteristics of local clay soils are evident. The saturated and sticky clay soils prohibit access into the wetlands by heavy equipment until the soils are almost completely dry. Earlier dewatering of some units is conducted so that there will be a dry enough substrate for maintenance.

None of the lands within Kern Refuge's approved boundary are designated Prime Farmland or Farmland of Statewide Importance by the California Department of Conservation.

Pixley Refuge
The eleven soils types that have been mapped within Pixley Refuge's approved boundary include: Akers-Akers, Saline-Sodic Complex (18.3 acres); Biggriz-Biggriz, Saline-Sodic Complex (101 acres); Gambogy loam (469 acres); Gambogy-Biggriz, Saline-Sodic Association (4,157 acres); Gareck-Garces Association (2,101 acres); Hanford sandy loam (less than 1 acre); Houser silty clay (15 acres); Kimberlina fine sandy loam (580 acres); Lethent silt loam (2,193 acres); Nahrub silt loam (74 acres); and Riverwash (less than 1 acre). All of these soils are alluvium

derived mainly from granitic rock sources located in former fan terraces, alluvial fans, flood plains, and basin rims.

With the exception of 300 to 600 acres of created wetlands that include levees and roads on Lethent silt loam within Pixley Refuge boundary, all of the other soil types have not been significantly disturbed. Less frequently used dirt roads occur along the boundaries and are used for periodic surveys and fence maintenance. The majority of the other soil types support introduced grasses. Grazing occurs on about 4,730 acres of Pixley Refuge to provide more suitable habitat for listed species and to promote the establishment and growth of native vegetation. No new development is planned for the Pixley Refuge, but periodic maintenance of the roads and wetlands is required.

More than 1,000 acres of land within the approved boundary have been leveled and reclaimed for irrigated croplands. Regular soil amendments are required to maintain productivity of cultivated crops. While Houser silty clay, Kimberlina fine sandy loam, Lethent silty loam, Nahrub silt loam, and Riverwash are not considered prime farmland, these soil types, with the exception of Riverwash, are farmed. However, about 340 acres are considered Farmland of Statewide Importance by the California Department of Conservation. The Department of Conservation defines Farmland of Statewide Importance as irrigated land similar to Prime Farmland that has a good combination of physical and chemical characteristics for the production of agricultural crops. This land has minor shortcomings, such as greater slopes or less ability to store soil moisture than Prime Farmland. Land must have been used for production of irrigated crops at some time during the four years prior to the mapping date.

Water

Kern Refuge

<u>Historic Environment.</u> Historically, the land area now managed as the Kern Refuge was at the extreme southern portion of Tulare Lake. The present-day location of Kern Refuge and the extent of the historic lake basin suggest that during wet years, areas of Kern Refuge may have been flooded by rising lake waters. Additionally, areas of Kern Refuge likely supported emergent wetland vegetation and riparian habitat that connected streams originating to the east in the Sierra Nevada Mountains with the historic Tulare Lake Basin in the Valley.

Conversion of the southern Valley from natural lands to agriculture beginning in the late 1800s resulted in the loss of wetlands and increased management of rivers to control floods and provide irrigation water to farmers. During this time, low dikes and canals were constructed for agricultural purposes on the land now occupied by the Kern Refuge and construction of the Goose Lake Canal, the major waterway that bisects the Refuge into eastern and western halves, was completed. With an average annual rainfall of six inches, the loss of natural wetlands, decreased frequency of spring floods, and a highly managed water delivery system of canals and dikes, the wetland dynamics of the southern Valley of today bears little resemblance to that of less than 100 years ago.

Refuge Water Development and Management. When development of the Kern Refuge began in the early 1960s, ten wells were drilled throughout the Refuge to provide a source of water for wetland management purposes. These wells averaged slightly in excess of 800 feet deep and were able to provide a limited source of water at a rate of approximately 1,600 gallons per minute. This production rate did not meet the needs of the Refuge's habitat and electrical costs prohibited the Service from using this groundwater as a sole source for habitat management.

Currently, three of the wells are still operable with water levels stabilized approximately 200 feet below the surface. Water quality is relatively good with the exception of boron and arsenic levels that are consistently high in all wells. Slightly below the ground surface and located above an impervious clay layer is a perched or suspended aquifer or layer of water that is highly saline and not suitable for irrigation or habitat purposes. In some locations around the Refuge, this perched aquifer is less than 5 feet below the surface.

Because using the wells proved to be cost prohibitive, the Service began purchasing fall and spring irrigation water from local water districts when available. In years of normal rainfall and when budgets permitted, sufficient water was purchased to flood less than 2,500 acres of fall and winter habitat at a cost exceeding $240,000. In years of limited water availability, less than 1,200 acres were flooded and this habitat was not available until late in the fall or early winter, far too late for the early fall migrant ducks that use the area.

The Central Valley Project Improvement Act, Title 34 of Public Law 102-575, was passed by Congress on October 30, 1992. A major purpose of the CVPIA was to change the management of the Central Valley Project to make fish, wildlife, and associated habitat protection and restoration a project purpose equivalent to that of supplying water and power for municipal and agricultural purposes. The CVPIA identified wetlands as a key component of wildlife protection and enhancement in the Central Valley and specified actions to further assess water needs and supply opportunities. Under provisions of the CVPIA, Kern Refuge was provided an annual allocation of 25,000 acre-feet of water for wetland management purposes.

Only since implementing the Central Valley Project Improvement Act of 1992 (CVPIA) has the amount of water delivered to the Kern Refuge been consistent and of sufficient volume to provide adequate wetland habitat for migratory waterfowl and waterbirds. With this water, the Refuge is able to flood 3,000 to 6,400 acres sequentially over a 3 to 5 month period beginning in mid-August. Normally all CVPIA water destined for the Refuge is released from the California Aqueduct into the Buena Vista Water Storage District system and transported nearly 12 miles through the Buena Vista Water Storage District Main Drain canal to the Refuge boundary.

The CVPIA water is divided into two categories, Level 2 supplies sustain the historic level of habitat produced annually on the Kern Refuge, and Level 4 supplies provide sufficient water to reach optimum development of all potential wetland habitat on the Refuge. The CVPIA allocated a total of 9,950 acre-feet of Level 2 water and 15,050 acre-feet of Level 4 water for developing and maintaining 6,700 acres of wetland habitat on an annual basis. Once water has been delivered into unit 1 of the Refuge, the water will be distributed throughout the moist soil units on the Refuge via a lift pump structure and a series of distribution ditches. Throughout the balance of the Refuge's seasonal wetlands, water will be distributed on a gravity flow basis through a system of pipes and gates that control these flows.

Early fall flood-up of Refuge habitat coincides with the late irrigations of agricultural crops upstream from the Refuge along the Main Drain/Goose Lake Canal. During this period, the Refuge water supply is heavily affected by irrigation return flows into the system. Water quality analysis during this period has shown no significant levels of pesticides, heavy metals, or other contaminants that could be detrimental to Refuge wildlife or habitat. However, high levels of dissolved salts have been documented. By mid-November, these agricultural return flows have ceased and water quality has greatly improved.

Flooding. In 1961, while searching for an adequate water supply for the Kern Refuge, the Service considered accepting floodwater from Poso Creek that originates in the southern Sierra Nevada Mountains. In 1962 and 1963, the Poso Creek channel was realigned and improved to handle 1,000 cubic feet per second of floodwater and extended to reach the southeast corner of the Refuge. No legal provisions were made to dispose of floodwater in excess of the holding capacity of the Refuge at any given time. Major floods originating from the Poso Creek watershed occur approximately every 10 to 12 years during which total discharges may exceed 130,000 acre-feet of water. Smaller floods generating in excess of 35,000 acre-feet of floodwater occur every four to five years.

Floods that reach the Refuge generally occur during the January through March period, the same time the Refuge has reached its maximum habitat management levels, thus limiting the amount of available floodwater storage capacity.

Because the Refuge is not on any natural watercourse, the Service has no discharge point that does not interfere with neighboring landowners. To release any water from the Refuge, prior approval from downstream users on Goose Lake Canal must be obtained. This is not an option during floods since other rivers and streams are usually in flood stage as well and the Poso Creek water would be an additional burden.

Aerial View of Kern Refuge Facing Southwest During 1986 Flood. U.S. Fish & Wildlife Service Photo.

Normal management practices for seasonal wetlands require that every unit be dewatered each spring to permit the growth of annual food plants. To facilitate the draining of Refuge impoundments water must be released from units 7 and 8 to provide space for other units to the south to be drained. In the past, this drain water has been given to adjacent landowners for use as irrigation water or to help create habitat on private wetlands.

Pixley Refuge
Situated within the historic flood plain of Deer Creek, the area now managed as the Pixley Refuge was on the eastern edge of Tulare Lake. While the far west portion of the Turkey Tract may have been a part of the actual wetlands of the lake, the majority of the remaining land area probably consisted of riparian habitat, seasonally flooded wetlands, vernal pools, and wet meadows, depending on the level of precipitation in any given year.

Although more than 750 acres of Pixley Refuge are designated to be managed as wetlands, sufficient water has not been available to provide any significant marsh habitat on a reliable basis. Infrequent flood flows in Deer Creek have at times been diverted into the Refuge wetlands to provide habitat on a very limited basis. In addition, in years of sufficient runoff when excess irrigation water is present, the Pixley Irrigation District has used some of the wetland units for groundwater recharge, providing habitat for water birds as a secondary benefit. While this habitat has been beneficial, this recharge water usually occurs in late spring and early summer, which is too late for the fall and winter migrant species to use the area.

With the passage of the CVPIA, the Pixley Refuge was provided an annual water allocation of 6,000 acre-feet including 1,280 acre-feet of Level 2 water and 4,720 acre-feet of Level 4 water. This allocation was intended to be sufficient to allow the development and maintenance of 755 acres of seasonal wetlands including 25 acres of riparian habitat, and 545 acres of irrigated pastures and croplands to be used primarily by lesser and greater sandhill cranes. While the designated source for the Refuge's CVPIA water allocation was the Friant-Kern Canal, no suitable canals or pipelines currently connect the Refuge to the water source.

As an interim measure to provide the Pixley Refuge with water while a delivery system can be developed, a deep well was drilled in 1994 as a joint project with Ducks Unlimited. With the water from this well, which is just west of County Road 88, east of the Pixley Refuge wetland units, the Pixley Refuge can develop and maintain approximately 300 acres of seasonal wetlands. Various alternatives have been considered for a permanent delivery conduit for a Friant-Kern water supply but the most promising is to use existing pipeline systems from the Friant-Kern Canal to a point west of Highway 99 and then construct a new line from there to the Refuge wetlands. It may be necessary to drill a second well on the Refuge as part of a conjunctive use program that will permit the combined use of wells and delivered surface water to meet the water needs of the Refuge. When the final delivery system is in place, total wetlands will exceed 750 acres, more than twice the current flooded acreage.

Air Quality

The Refuges are in California's San Joaquin Valley Air Basin. Air quality in the Valley is among the worst in the United States. The San Joaquin Valley Unified Air Pollution Control District is the agency responsible for ensuring compliance with Federal and State air quality standards in the Valley. The Federal and State governments have each established ambient air quality standards for several pollutants. Most standards have been set to protect public health. However, standards for some pollutants are based on other values such as protecting crops and materials and avoiding nuisance conditions. Currently, the Valley is federally classified as a serious nonattainment area for both ground-level ozone and particulate matter less than 10 microns in diameter (PM10). In addition, the Valley is classified as a severe nonattainment area for the California ozone standard and nonattainment for the PM10 standard. The Valley is in attainment or has not been classified for all other criteria pollutants.

Ozone, the main component of photochemical smog, is formed through a complex series of chemical reactions between reactive organic gasses (ROG) and nitrogen oxides (NOx). On-road motor vehicles are the largest contributors to NOx emissions in the Valley. On-road motor vehicles, area-wide sources, and stationary sources are significant contributors to ROG emissions. A significant portion of the stationary source ROG emissions are fugitive emissions from the extensive oil and gas production operations in the southern Valley. Once formed, ozone remains in the atmosphere for one or two days. As a result, ozone is a regional pollutant and often affects a large area. Ozone's main effects include damage to vegetation, chemical deterioration of various materials, and irritation and damage to the human respiratory system.

Carbon monoxide (CO) is a odorless, invisible gas which usually forms as a by-product of incomplete combustion of organic substances. The majority of the CO emitted in the Valley comes from motor vehicles. Carbon monoxide is a relatively localized pollutant, often resulting from a combination of high traffic volumes and traffic congestion. As a result, measured concentrations are not necessarily representative of the entire study area. A mildly toxic pollutant, CO interferes with oxygen transport to body tissues.

Airborne dust (PM10) is produced by stationary point sources such as: fuel combustion and industrial processes; fugitive sources, such as roadway dust from paved and unpaved roads; wind erosion from open land; and transportation sources, such as automobiles. The primary sources of PM10 in the Valley are fugitive dust from paved and unpaved roads and agricultural operations. Soil type and soil moisture content are important factors in PM10 emissions. Federal and State PM10 standards are designed to prevent respiratory disease and protect visibility.

Certain land uses are considered more sensitive to air pollution than others. Locations such as schools, hospitals, and convalescent homes are labeled sensitive receptors because their occupants (the young, old, and infirm) are more susceptible to respiratory infections and other air quality-related health problems than the general public. Residential areas are also considered sensitive receptors because residents tend to be home for extended periods, resulting in sustained exposure to any pollutants present. Sensitive receptors in the study area include the Refuge Complex headquarters and residences at Kern Refuge and the few scattered private residences south and east of Pixley Refuge.

Plant Communities

Kern Refuge

The Kern Refuge supports a variety of wetland and upland vegetation over the 10,618 acres managed for waterfowl and endangered species. The 1986 Master Plan identified six major vegetative communities (marsh/seasonal wetland, alkali playa, valley grassland, cultivated cropland, alkali scrub, and riparian) with 16 subcategories. At that time, wetland acreage was based on the amount of wetland habitat that was normally flooded from 1977 to 1984. From this information, wetland habitat accounted for approximately 37 percent (3,850 acres) of the total land area on the Refuge.

In recent years, the quantity and availability of water has increased, allowing the Kern Refuge to provide more wetland habitat. As part of the CCP process, a new vegetation map was completed that more accurately reflects current conditions on the Refuge. Vegetation types were delineated based on recent aerial photographs, global positioning system (GPS) data taken in the field, and additional ground truthing.

Based on this information, eight plant communities have been identified including grassland, seasonal marsh, alkali playa, grassland/alkali playa, moist soil wetland, riparian, valley sink scrub, and salt cedar (Figure 8). The salt cedar plant community covers approximately 1,600 acres and is in former wetland and grassland habitat types. Wetland habitat covers approximately 5,300 acres and includes 3,800 acres of seasonal marsh, 1,200 acres of moist soil wetlands, and 215 acres of riparian habitat. An additional 1,200 acres of moist soil wetlands are being restored.

Salt cedar is most commonly found on the west side of the Kern Refuge in dense impenetrable stands. Stands on the east side occur in seasonal wetlands and along the levees of some wetland units. On both sides of the Refuge, this habitat type has replaced grassland and wetland habitat. The Service is actively using mechanical and chemical control methods in an effort to control and remove this invasive species to restore wetland and grassland habitats.

All plant community names are from Terrestrial Natural Communities of California (Holland 1986). Exceptions include moist soil wetlands and agricultural croplands. Appendix E includes a list of plant species documented on the Refuge.

<u>Wetland Plant Communities</u>. Wetland plant communities occur in seasonal marshes, moist soil wetlands, and in riparian habitat. Salt cedar habitat occurs in these three wetland habitat types.

Seasonal Marsh. Units 1, 1A, 2, 2A, 3, 6B, 6C, 7, and 8 are designated seasonal marshes and cover approximately 3,800 acres. They are large (156 to 846 acres) units characterized by water depths less than 4 feet and robust perennial wetland vegetation. Even though these units are

Seasonal Marsh Habitat at Kern Refuge. U.S. Fish & Wildlife Service Photo.

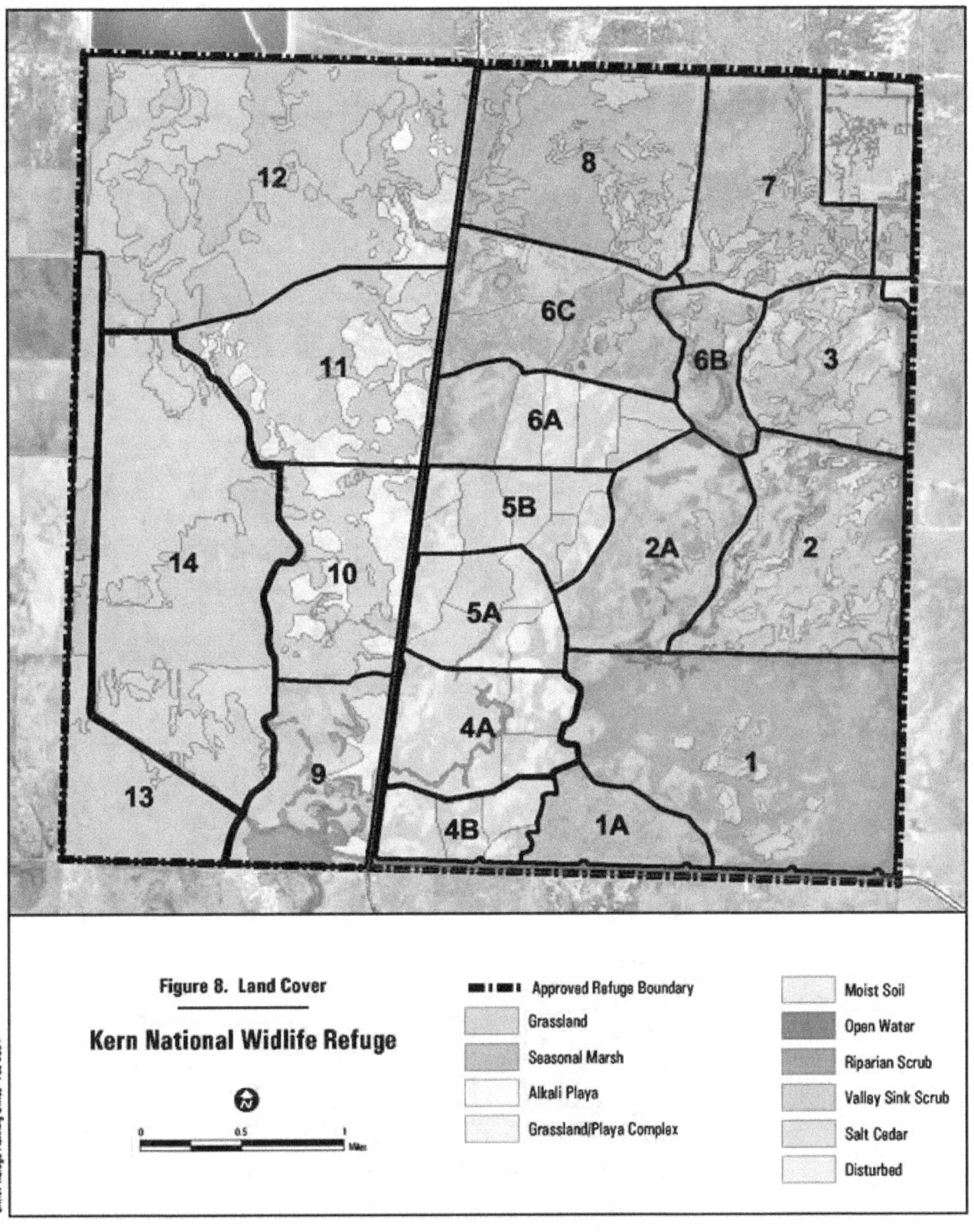

Figure 8. Land Cover

Kern National Widlife Refuge

CA/NV Refuge Planning Office · Feb 2004

0   0.5   1 Miles

Legend:
- ▬ ▮ ▬ Approved Refuge Boundary
- Grassland
- Seasonal Marsh
- Alkali Playa
- Grassland/Playa Complex
- Moist Soil
- Open Water
- Riparian Scrub
- Valley Sink Scrub
- Salt Cedar
- Disturbed

seasonally flooded only from September to May or June, adequate soil moisture throughout the dry and hot summer months provides suitable conditions for growing and maintaining cattail and hardstem bulrush. While cattail and hardstem bulrush may dominate certain areas of some seasonal marshes, other wetland plants are also common and include alkali bulrush and spike-rush. In deeper areas, burrhead and arrowhead are common, especially along the edges of ditches. Woody vegetation within these marshes can occur as isolated trees and shrubs of salt cedar, willow, and cottonwood or in dense thickets (salt cedar). Patches of iodine bush and alkali heath occur in slightly higher areas within the units. Selected areas may be occasionally mowed, disked, or burned to control perennial vegetation and maintain open water habitat.

Moist Soil Wetlands. Units 4, 5, 6A, and 14 are designated moist soil wetlands and include about 2,400 acres. These wetlands are also seasonally flooded, small (22 to 62 acres), and are characterized by water depths less than 8 inches in the fall and winter and less than 2 inches in spring. These units are intensely managed by the Service through mowing, disking, and burning to maximize waterfowl food plant production. In any given year, approximately 20 percent of the total moist soil wetland acreage is subject to some form of vegetation management. These management actions are to promote the growth of swamp timothy and water grass while curtailing the spread of alkali bulrush and isolated stands of cattail and hardstem bulrush. Other species existing in these units include sprangle-top and various species of rushes. Swamp timothy exists naturally and requires one or two irrigations in the late spring or early summer while water grass is directly cultivated in prepared units and irrigated as needed.

Riparian Habitat. Unit 9 and the southern portion of unit 10 contain the largest tract (215 acres) of riparian habitat on the Kern Refuge. The riparian habitat on the Refuge is contiguous with riparian habitat

Riparian Habitat on Kern Refuge. U.S. Fish & Wildlife Service Photo.

immediately south of the Refuge on private property. Viewed from above, a series of old channels associated with the Kern River meander through this area from south to north. Water is managed in these units to maintain and promote this habitat type on the Refuge but there is no outlet. Cottonwood and willow trees dominate but salt cedar is common in some areas. Smartweed is common in the channels.

Alkali Playa. Easily distinguishable mostly bare, alkali soils. The most common plants associated with alkali playas are annual *Atriplex* species and annual grasses.

Upland Plant Communities. Upland plant communities occur in grasslands, alkali playas, grassland/alkali playa complex, and valley sink scrub. Salt cedar habitat exists in the following four upland habitat types.

Grasslands. This habitat type covers approximately 2,800 acres on the west side of the Kern Refuge occurring from the southern to northern boundaries. Depending on the soil type and elevation, grassland plants are associated with clay and sandy soils, and where the elevation is slightly lower, with vernal pools. Common vernal pool plants include coyote-thistle, Fremont's goldfields, and short woollyheads. These plants can be found in or near vernal pools were shallow pools and meandering sloughs collect moisture from winter rains. Both sandy and clay soil grassland plants may occur as either dense or sparse associations of brome, barley, annual fescue, California poppy, cream cups, bird's eye gilia, spikeweed, and goldfields. Nonnative grasses (bromes and fescues) can become dense over a considerable area and encroach into areas supporting mainly native grasses as well as decrease the overall suitability of grassland habitat for threatened and endangered species. As a result, grazing is used to control nonnative grasses and to provide more open habitat suitable to the endangered blunt-nosed leopard lizard and Tipton kangaroo rat.

Grassland/Alkali Playa Complex. This community consisted of areas where alkali playa and grassland habitats were interspersed and could not be delineated. Cumulatively, the alkali playa and the grassland/alkali playa complex covers approximately 500 acres on the Kern Refuge.

Valley Sink Scrub. This habitat type occurs mainly on the west side, but small patches occur in higher areas in seasonal wetlands on the east side. Approximately 750 acres of this habitat type occur on the Kern Refuge and may be dominated by either saltbush or iodine bush. Saltbush-dominated areas are sparsely vegetated and may also include aster. Plants in iodine bush–dominated communities are mostly succulent and occur on alkaline or poorly drained soils. Common plants in this community are iodine bush, suaeda, and alkali heath.

Pixley Refuge
Eight major land cover categories are found within the Pixley Refuge approved boundary: California annual grassland, alkali playa, northern

claypan vernal pool, valley saltbush scrub, riparian, Great Valley willow scrub, intensively managed moist soil units, and agricultural croplands. About 74 percent of the lands within the approved boundary are annual grassland. Of the wetland plant communities, managed moist soil communities cover the greatest area. Figure 9 shows the distribution of plant communities within the approved refuge boundary. Below is a description of each plant community, including plant composition, ecological relationships, and distribution on the Refuge.

Wetland Plant Communities.

Moist Soil Wetlands. All the 756 acres of managed wetlands on the Pixley Refuge are designated moist soil wetlands. These small wetlands are seasonally flooded and characterized by water depths of less than eight inches in the fall and winter and less than two inches in the spring. These units are occasionally managed by the Refuge through mowing, disking, and burning to maximize waterfowl food plant production. In any given year, less than 20 percent of the total moist soil wetland acreage is subject to some form of vegetation or soil management. These management actions are to promote the growth of swamp timothy and water grass while curtailing the spread of alkali bulrush and isolated stands of cattail and hardstem bulrush. Other species occurring in these units include sprangle-top and various species of rushes. Swamp timothy exists naturally and requires one or two irrigations in the late spring/early summer while water grass is directly cultivated in prepared units and irrigated as needed.

Riparian. This habitat type is limited (about 15 acres) and occurs in a narrow band along Deer Creek on the southern border of the Pixley Refuge. Scattered cottonwood and willow trees are found along this creek.

Alkali Playa. This community occupies about 39 acres, or less than 1 percent, of Pixley Refuge. However, these figures are an underestimate, because only the larger alkali playas were mapped. About 1,300 acres of the area mapped as annual grassland contain numerous small playas interspersed throughout. This community occurs on poorly drained soils with high salinity and/or alkalinity due to water evaporation that accumulates in closed drainages. Typically, vegetative cover in this community is 70 percent or less and the soil has a white salt crust. Indicator species of this community include alkali plagiobothrys, salt sand-spurry, low barley, Mediterranean grass, and alkali weed (Trask 1989).

Northern Claypan Vernal Pool. Northern claypan vernal pools are shallow depressions lined with an impervious clay layer that temporarily fill with water during the winter and spring rains and dry out completely during the summer. Water stands in the pool during the early part of the growing season, preventing most grassland species from becoming established. However, several annual plant species are specially adapted to this unique environment. Plants commonly found in vernal pools at Pixley Refuge include goldfields, popcorn flower, coyote thistle, mousetail, pillwort, woolly heads, pygmy-weed, and flowering quillwort.

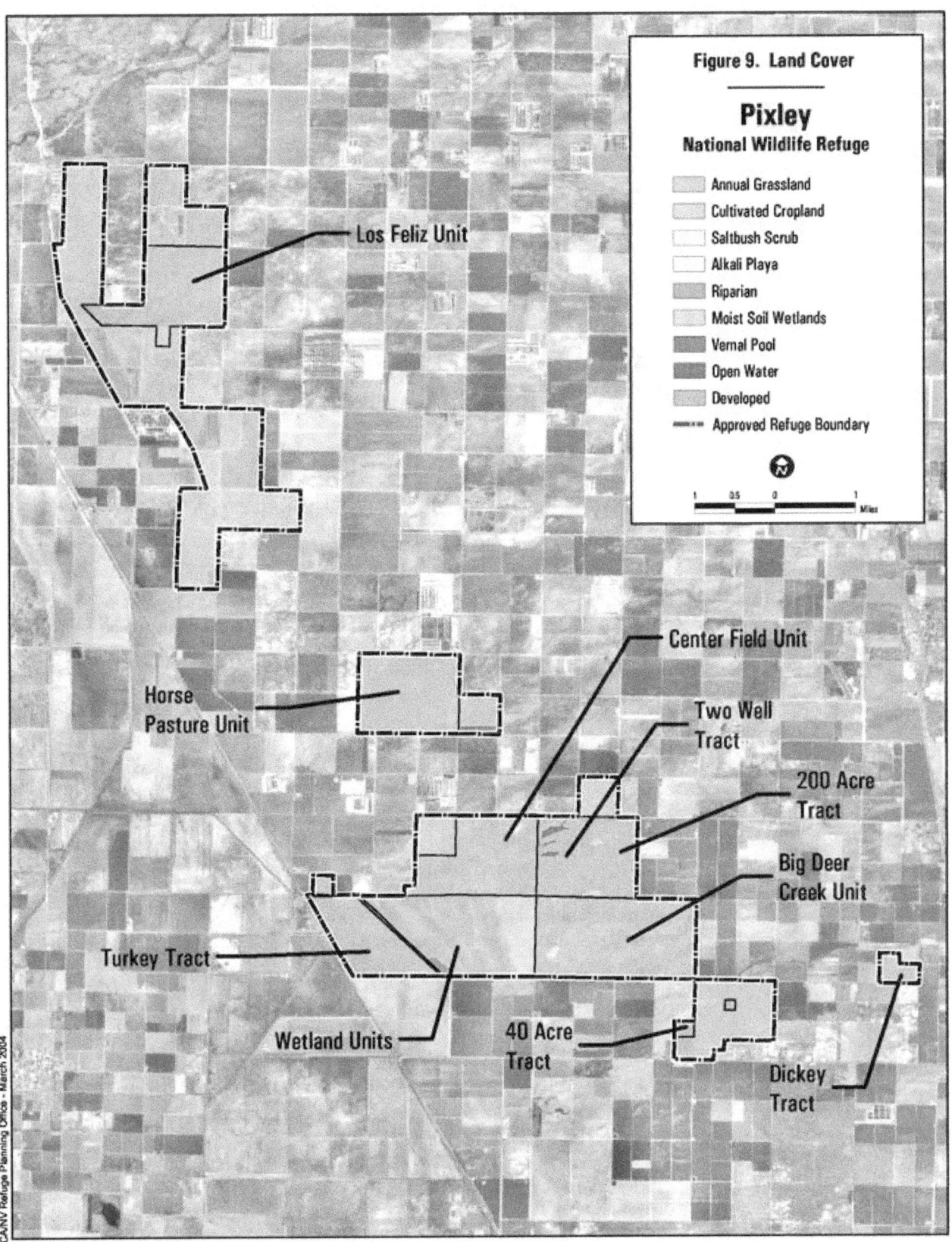

Figure 9. Land Cover

Pixley
National Wildlife Refuge

- Annual Grassland
- Cultivated Cropland
- Saltbush Scrub
- Alkali Playa
- Riparian
- Moist Soil Wetlands
- Vernal Pool
- Open Water
- Developed
- — — Approved Refuge Boundary

Los Feliz Unit

Center Field Unit

Two Well Tract

200 Acre Tract

Big Deer Creek Unit

Horse Pasture Unit

Turkey Tract

Wetland Units

40 Acre Tract

Dickey Tract

CA/NV Refuge Planning Office - March 2004

Vernal Pool at Pixley Refuge. U.S. Fish & Wildlife Service Photo.

On Pixley Refuge, vernal pools are found only on the Two Well Tract and the Big Deer Creek Unit and total about 36 acres.

<u>Upland Plant Communities</u>.
California Annual Grassland. Approximately 7,347 acres, or 74 percent, of the lands within the approved Pixley Refuge boundary are California annual grassland. This grassland is a mosaic of grassland and alkali playas with vernal pools scattered throughout. The grasslands on Pixley Refuge are typically dominated by nonnative annual grasses including foxtail barley, low barley, soft chess, and red brome. Common forbs in this community include red-stemmed filaree, California burclover, bush seepweed, common spikeweed, bird's eye gilia, and alkali heath. Alkali goldenbush (a shrub) is also occasionally found in the grasslands. Soil type has an important influence on the composition and structure of the grassland community. In general, grassland plants growing on fine textured soils are less dense and smaller than those growing on coarse textered soils. The grasslands along Deer Creek have more coarse textured soils and probably receive some subsurface moisture. Clumps of the perennial grass alkali sacaton are common in this area (Trask 1989).

When rainfall is sufficient, cattle are grazed on the grasslands to reduce cover and improve habitat conditions for the blunt-nosed leopard lizard and Tipton kangaroo rat. All of Pixley Refuge uplands are grazed except a 20-foot by 20-foot exclosure constructed in 1975 in the southwestern corner of Section 23.

Valley Saltbush Scrub. This community is found in the 246-acre area just east of the managed wetland units and was set aside as mitigation for the development of the wetlands. Dominant shrubs in this community include saltbush, iodine bush, and suaeda. The understory is composed primarily of the same nonnative annual grass and forb species found in the annual grasslands.

Agricultural Croplands. About 1,058 acres of private land within the approved Pixley Refuge acquisition boundary are actively farmed to provide feed for several dairies adjacent to the Refuge. These lands are subject to intensive farming (discing, soil amendments, irrigating, and harvesting) to support alfalfa and grain production.

Developed Areas. A number of dairies have developed within the approved acquisition boundary since Pixley Refuge was established. These dairies now occupy about 704 acres within the approved boundary.

Wildlife

The variety of unique habitats at the Refuges support a diversity of wildlife species. More than 359 species of birds, mammals, amphibians, and reptiles have been documented on the Refuges. Some 15 special-status wildlife species are known or believed to use the Refuges. Appendix E contains a list of wildlife species observed in the Refuges.

Birds.

Kern Refuge. A total of 214 bird species have been sighted on Kern Refuge. Fifty-nine different species have nested on the Refuge. Species recorded on the Refuge include waterbirds, such as northern pintails, green-winged teal, and northern shoveler, which account for the largest number of ducks wintering on the Refuge. Other species including mallards, American wigeon, gadwall, cinnamon teal, canvasbacks, redheads, lesser scaups, ring-necked ducks, buffleheads, and ruddy ducks; and Canada geese, white-fronted geese, white pelicans, double-crested cormorants, belted kingfishers, egrets, herons, American and least bitterns, grebes, rails, gulls, terns, plovers, black-necked stilts,

Avocet Chick. U.S. Fish & Wildlife Service Photo.

American avocets, greater yellowlegs, western and least sandpipers, dunlins, and long-billed dowitchers also use Kern Refuge.

Raptors, such as red-tailed hawks, northern harriers, Swainson's hawks, golden eagles, peregrine falcons, kestrels, barn owls, burrowing owls, and great-horned owls, have been observed on Kern Refuge.

On Kern Refuge, west of Goose Lake Canal, there are about 2,600 acres of upland communities consisting of annual grasslands and shrubs, such as iodine bush, saltbush, and seepweed. These flats have also been invaded by salt cedar. In some areas, small, sometimes-circular alkali flats exist. These areas and some of the higher areas scattered throughout the Refuge and along levees, provide habitat for birds adapted to an upland existence including ring-necked pheasants, mourning doves, and turkey vultures.

Other birds found in the uplands or in vegetation on the edges of wetlands include hummingbirds, swallows, horned larks, flycatchers, crows, ravens, and sparrows.

In the spring and fall a variety of neotropical migratory birds can be found in the riparian areas of the Kern Refuge. Some of the species include, common yellowthroats, western tanagers, warblers, vireos, kinglets, thrushes, and cedar waxwings.

Red-winged, tricolored, and Brewer's blackbirds use the marshes.

Pixley Refuge. Many of the same species that use Kern Refuge use Pixley Refuge. Since Pixley Refuge consists primarily of the Valley Grassland plant community type, mostly grassland bird species nest on the Refuge. In recent years, beginning in August, ground water is pumped to the surface to provide about 300 acres of moist-soil habitat types. This provides habitat for migrating and wintering birds. Sandhill cranes are the most prominent species that roost on Pixley Refuge wetlands. Cranes begin arriving in September and numbers may peak at up to 6,000 birds in January. Sixty-seven species of birds have been documented using Pixley Refuge.

In the fall and winter, the wetlands also support many of the same dabbling ducks found at Kern Refuge. In the past five years, green-winged teal, northern shovelers, and mallards have been the three most abundant ducks counted during mid-winter aerial surveys. Other wintering waterfowl species abundant on the Refuge include gadwalls, wigeons, and northern pintails. Wintering ducks may reach numbers as high as 6,000 to 8,000 birds. Wintering Canada geese may number as high as 600 birds and smaller flocks of white-fronted and snow geese may be present.

Great Egrets. U.S. Fish & Wildlife Service Photo.

Pixley Refuge also provides wintering habitat for white-faced ibis. In recent years, more than 2,000 white-faced ibis have been counted in a single day roosting in the wetlands. Wintering and migrating shorebirds also use the Refuge. Some of the more common shorebirds include: black-necked stilts, yellowlegs, American avocets, killdeer, long-billed dowitchers, and western and least sandpipers. Occasionally marbled godwits and Wilson's phalaropes are observed. In the uplands, long-billed curlews are frequently sited in the winter, but mountain plovers are rarely observed. Waterbirds that may be observed at the Refuge include American coots, pied-billed grebes, various species of gulls, as well as wading birds, such as great blue herons, black-crowned night herons, great and snowy egrets, and American bitterns. Raptors observed on the Refuge include red-tailed hawks, northern harriers, American kestrels, burrowing owls, barn owls, and occasional sightings of great horned owls, prairie falcons, peregrine falcons, black-shouldered kites, turkey vultures, and Cooper's hawks. Other common birds include mourning doves, western meadow larks, horned larks, loggerhead shrikes, and various species of sparrows and blackbirds.

Mammals
Kern Refuge. A total of 27 species of mammals have been sighted on Kern Refuge. An additional 14 species may exist there based on their regional distribution; however, sightings have not been confirmed. Some of the mammals found on the Refuge include desert cottontail, black-tailed jackrabbit, coyote, kit fox, bobcat, opossum, raccoon, muskrat, beaver, badger, long-tailed weasel, striped and western spotted skunk, California voles, Heermann's kangaroo rat, Tipton kangaroo rat, deer mouse, western harvest mouse, the San Joaquin pocket mouse, Botta's pocket gopher, house mouse, roof rat, the endangered Buena Vista Lake shrew, California ground squirrel, and the San Joaquin antelope ground squirrel. The Refuge may also be home to the broad-handed (California) mole, although this is unconfirmed.

The Refuge is home to at least two flying mammals, the Mexican free-tailed bat and the western mastiff bat. In addition, several other species of bats may forage for insects on the Refuge including the western small-footed myotis, California myotis, Yuma myotis, silver-haired bat, western pipistrelle, big brown bat, hoary bat, western red bat, Townsend's western big-eared bat, and pallid bat.

Pixley Refuge. At least 16 species of mammals use Pixley Refuge as habitat, and another 8 species may exist on the Refuge but their presence has not yet been confirmed. Of the 16 mammals known to inhabit Pixley Refuge, 5 are carnivores, such as coyotes, endangered San Joaquin kit foxes, badgers, striped skunks, and long-tailed weasels. Other species present include black-tailed jackrabbits, Audubon cottontail (desert cottontail), California ground squirrel (Beechey ground squirrel), Botta's pocket gopher (valley pocket gopher), the endangered Tipton kangaroo rat, Heermann's kangaroo rat, deer mice, western harvest mice, house mice, and, on rare occasions, in the water delivery canals, muskrats. Species that may be on the Refuge but their presence has not been confirmed include western mastiff bats, Mexican free-tailed bats, ornate shrews, broad-handed (California) moles, raccoons, spotted skunks, San Joaquin antelope ground squirrels, and California voles.

Reptiles and Amphibians
Kern Refuge. Kern Refuge is home to 12 species of reptiles and 4 species of amphibians.

The four species of lizards that inhabit Kern Refuge are the blunt-nosed leopard lizard, an endangered species, the coast horned lizard, California side-blotched lizard, and Western (California) whiptail.

Seven species of snakes have been recorded using the Refuge. One species, the western (northern Pacific) rattlesnake is venomous. This pit viper is commonly seen in the spring when temperatures begin rising. The remaining species are the Pacific gopher snake, California (common) kingsnake, western long-nosed snake, California glossy snake, southwestern black-headed snake, and the common garter snake. An eighth species, the coachwhip (San Joaquin whipsnake) (*Masticophis flagellum ruddocki*) exists in the vicinity of the Refuge and possibly exists on the Refuge but this has not been confirmed.

One western pond turtle was found on the Kern Refuge in the early nineties, but that was a rare occurrence. The Service's practice of draining wetlands in the summer to prevent avian botulism probably keeps the western pond turtle from being a permanent resident on the Refuge. This species possibly could thrive here if fresh water was available year around.

The amphibians found on Kern Refuge include the Pacific treefrog, bullfrog, western toad, and western spadefoot toad.

<u>Pixley Refuge.</u> Pixley Refuge provides habitat for 13 species of reptiles and amphibians and another 3 species of reptiles possibly exist on the Refuge, but their presence has not yet been confirmed.

The four species of lizards inhabiting Pixley Refuge are the endangered blunt-nosed lizard, coast horned lizard, California side-blotched lizard, and western (California) whiptails. Western fence lizards may exist on the Refuge but their presence has not yet been confirmed.

The five species of snakes present on the Refuge are the Pacific gopher snake, California (common) kingsnake, western long-nosed snake, southwestern black-headed snake, and, one poisonous species, the western (northern Pacific) rattlesnake. The San Joaquin whipsnake (coachwhip) and the California glossy snake possibly inhabit the Refuge but confirmations have not been made for these two species.

Pacific Treefrog. U.S. Fish & Wildlife Service Photo.

The four species of amphibians that inhabit Pixley Refuge are the Pacific treefrog, western (California) toad, western (Pacific) spadefoot toad, and bullfrog.

Invertebrates
<u>Kern Refuge.</u> Even though aquatic invertebrates are no doubt important as food for many species of wetland wildlife, there have been no comprehensive invertebrate surveys conducted at Kern Refuge.

Some surveys are done on occasion by researchers looking for a particular group of invertebrates. For example, when there is water on the Refuge, the Kern Mosquito and Vector Control District monitors the wet areas primarily for the seven species of mosquitoes that exist on the Refuge (*Culex erythrothorax, C. pipiens, C. tarsalis, Orahlerdatus dorsalis, O. melanimon, O. nigromaculis,* and *Aedes vexans*). In a study of the feeding ecology of northern pintail and green-winged teal, Euliss and Harris (1987) sampled the esophagial contents of numerous ducks and found water fleas (Cladocera), seed shrimp, snails (Gastropoda), dragonflies and damselflies (Odonata), midges, and flower flies (Syrphidae). In another example, one researcher documented, for the first time, a species of cattail bug found in the pistillate heads or spikes of cattails growing on the Refuge.

During a 1997 limited survey for fairy shrimp, conducted in some of the alkali pools in the northeastern part of unit 12, one species was found.

Comprehensive surveys of invertebrate and crustacean species and learning more about their ecology are two areas that need further development at the Refuge.

Pixley Refuge. There have been no comprehensive surveys for invertebrates conducted at Pixley Refuge although aquatic invertebrates are no doubt an important source of food for many species of wetland wildlife.

During wet winters, several vernal pools collect and hold water. Three species of fairy shrimp have been identified in some of these pools. They include the versatile fairy shrimp, the alkali fairy shrimp, and the Federally threatened vernal pool fairy shrimp. Also, clam shrimp have been found in some of these pools but the species has not been identified.

Moth surveys conducted from 1993 to 1995 identified 55 species of moths on the Refuge.

Special Status Species

The following section provides more information on special status species that may exist or are known to exist on Kern or Pixley Refuges. This includes species that are in the following categories: Federally listed and proposed listed species; Bird Species of Conservation Concern at the Regional (U.S. Fish and Wildlife Service Pacific Region) or more local Bird Conservation Region (Coastal California Bird Conservation Region[1]) scale; and State listed species. Birds identified by the Service as species of conservation concern are predominantly nongame birds in need of conservation action to prevent future listing as an endangered species. Under Executive Order 13186 these species represent conservation priorities for the Service, and other Federal agencies, and are to be specifically considered during planning and when actions are proposed on Federal lands.

San Joaquin Kit Fox

The San Joaquin kit fox (*Vulpes macroti mutica*) is a small fox with relatively large ears and a long, bushy, black-tipped tail. They are endemic to the Valley and surrounding foothills and a few interior coast range watersheds. The San Joaquin kit fox is listed as a Federal and State endangered species.

---

[1] The Coastal California Bird Conservation Region includes the Central Valley and California coast south of San Francisco Bay.

San Joaquin Kit Fox. U.S. Fish & Wildlife Service Photo.

The San Joaquin kit fox is commonly associated with valley sink scrub, valley saltbush scrub, and annual grassland. Kit foxes also exist in some highly modified landscapes including petroleum fields, urban areas, and areas adjacent to agricultural fields. In general, they prefer to den in loose-textured soils but can be found on nearly every soil type (Service 1998). The San Joaquin kit fox's diet varies depending on abundance of potential food sources. Nocturnal rodents such as kangaroo rats, pocket mice, and white-footed mice comprise about one-third or more of their diet. Kit foxes also feed on California ground squirrel, black-tailed jackrabbit, San Joaquin antelope squirrel, desert cottontail, ground-nesting birds, and insects (Service 1998). Home ranges of kit fox vary, depending on prey abundance, from less than one square-mile up to twelve square-miles (Service 1998).

The primary threats to the survival of this species are loss and degradation of habitat by agricultural and industrial development and urbanization.

Population numbers are low on the Refuge with only seven kit foxes sighted on Kern Refuge during night spotlight surveys conducted from 1996 through 2000. Fifteen kit foxes were sighted on Pixley Refuge during this same time. Resident or denning kit fox have not been confirmed on Kern Refuge. Kit fox den sites were confirmed on Pixley Refuge prior to the wet winters of the mid-1990s when their prey population numbers crashed. Denning has not been confirmed since that time. Occasionally, kit fox are found dead on the roads near both Refuges.

Tipton Kangaroo Rat

The Tipton kangaroo rat (*Dipodomys nitratoides nitratoides*) is a small, buff-colored rodent endemic to the southern Valley. This species is listed as a Federal and State endangered species.

Tipton kangaroo rats inhabit arid-land communities such as iodine bush shrubland, valley saltbush scrub, and annual grassland on the floor of the Tulare Basin in level or nearly level terrain. Their habitat is typically characterized by one or more species of sparsely scattered woody shrubs and a ground cover of mostly introduced annual grasses and forbs. Shrubs typically associated with Tipton kangaroo rats are: spiny and common saltbushes, arrowscale, quailbush, iodine bush, pale-leaf goldenbush, honey mesquite, and seepweed. Much of the low-lying habitat occupied by Tipton kangaroo rats is susceptible to flooding from winter rains and overbank flooding from creeks. Tipton kangaroo rats commonly burrow in slightly elevated mounds, road berms, canal embankments, railroad beds, and the bases of shrubs and trees where windblown soils accumulate. The Tipton kangaroo rat's diet consists mostly of seeds with smaller amounts of green herbaceous vegetation and insects (Service 1998).

Tipton Kangaroo Rat. U.S. Fish & Wildlife Service Photo.

In the past, the primary reason for the Tipton kangaroo rat's decline was habitat loss due to agricultural conversion. Today, the greatest threats to this species are habitat destruction or modification from industrial and agriculturally-related development, cultivation, buildup of heavy thatch by nonnative annual grasses, and urbanization. Flooding also poses a threat to this species (Service 1998).

Pixley Refuge provides some of the best remaining habitat for Tipton kangaroo rats (Service 1998). The Endangered Species Recovery Program has been studying the population ecology of Tipton kangaroo rats at Pixley Refuge since 1992. Surveys are conducted on a grid in the Deer Creek East Unit twice a year. Few or no animals have been trapped in recent years. Population numbers crashed on Pixley Refuge and other areas of the southern Valley in the mid-1990s when the areas were flooded two winters in a row. Tipton kangaroo rats historically occurred in the upland communities on the west side of Kern Refuge. All of the west side was flooded in 1983 and partially flooded in the mid-1990s. In limited, small mammal live-trapping surveys, conducted in 1992, 1993, 1994, and 1998, few Tipton kangaroo rats were captured on the west side or near unit 8 on the east side.

Blunt-Nosed Leopard Lizard

The blunt-nosed leopard lizard (*Gambelia sila*) is a large lizard from the iguana family with a long tail, long powerful hind limbs, and a short, blunt snout. It is endemic to the Valley. The blunt-nosed leopard lizard is listed as a Federal and State endangered species.

Blunt-nosed leopard lizards are found in open, sparsely vegetated areas of low relief in the Valley and the surrounding foothills. In the Valley, this species is most commonly associated with nonnative grassland and valley sink scrub communities. Valley needlegrass grassland and alkali playa also provide habitat for this species. In the foothills, the blunt-nosed leopard lizard is found in saltbush scrub, upper Sonoran subshrub scrub, and serpentine bunchgrass. They generally use small rodent burrows for shelter from predators and temperature extremes (Service 1998). Blunt-nosed leopard lizards feed mostly on insects (primarily grasshoppers, crickets, and moths) and other lizards (Service 1998). Home ranges for this species vary from 0.25 acres to 2.7 acres for females and from 0.52 acres to 4.2 acres for males (Service 1998).

Blunt-Nosed Leopard Lizard. US Fish and Wildlife Service Photo.

The primary threats to blunt-nosed leopard lizards are habitat disturbance, destruction, and fragmentation. These threats come from a variety of sources including development and operation of oil and gas facilities, overgrazing, pesticide use, and on and off road vehicle use in or near blunt-nosed leopard lizard habitat (Service 1998).

On Pixley Refuge, Uptain et al. (1985) found densities of blunt-nosed leopard lizards ranging from 0.1 to 4.2 per acre. Biologists from California State University, Stanislaus's Endangered Species Recovery Program have been monitoring population numbers in the Deer Creek East Unit of Pixley Refuge from 1993 to the present. Population numbers experienced a drastic decline in the mid-nineties when there were successive years of high amounts of rainfall. On Pixley Refuge, lizard abundances appeared to be greater in the year 2000 monitoring season than they had been in recent years. On Kern Refuge, blunt-nosed leopard lizard surveys of limited scope were conducted on the west side in 1996 and 1998, with no blunt-nosed leopard lizards observed. The most recent sighting was one lizard on the east side of Kern Refuge in 1994. Four sightings occurred in 1993, three lizards on the east side and one in the San Joaquin Desert Research Natural Area (RNA) on the west side.

San Joaquin Antelope Squirrel

The San Joaquin antelope squirrel (*Ammospermophilus nelsoni*) is a small buff/tan colored ground squirrel with a light stripe on its side and a light grey or white belly. This species is endemic to the Valley and the Carrizo and Elkhorn Plains to the west. The San Joaquin antelope squirrel is listed as a Federal species of concern and a State threatened species.

The San Joaquin antelope squirrel inhabits arid annual grassland and shrubland communities. This species is most abundant in areas with sparse to moderate shrub cover (Service 1998). In the southern and western Valley, San Joaquin antelope squirrels are associated with plant communities containing saltbush and ephedra (Service 1998). They rarely occur on alkaline soils or in areas that are subject to flooding. San Joaquin antelope squirrels are omnivorous. They eat green vegetation, fungi, insects, and to a lesser extent, seeds (Service 1998).

The greatest threat to the San Joaquin antelope squirrel is loss of habitat to agricultural developments, urbanization, and petroleum extraction. The long-term effects of overgrazing, namely loss of shrub cover and soil erosion, may also threaten this species.

The San Joaquin antelope squirrel has not been seen on Kern Refuge for many years. The last confirmed sighting on Pixley Refuge was in 1985. San Joaquin antelope squirrels are more numerous south of Kern Refuge in the Elk Hills area.

Buena Vista Lake Shrew

The Buena Vista Lake shrew (*Sorex ornatus relictus*) is a mouse-sized mammal with a long snout and tiny bead-like eyes. The fur on its upper surface is blackish-brown and the lower surface is smoke gray. Its tail is bicolored and relatively short. Buena Vista Lake shrews were likely historically distributed throughout the Tulare Basin (Service 2000). This species is a Federally listed endangered species and a State species of special concern.

Buena Vista Lake shrews prefer moist habitats with an abundant layer of leaf litter. Plants typically found in their habitat include Fremont cottonwood, willows, glasswort, alkali heath, wild rye grass, and Baltic rush. The feeding and foraging habits of the Buena Vista Lake shrew are not known. In general, shrews feed mostly on insects and other invertebrates (Service 1998).

The primary reasons for the Buena Vista Lake shrew's historical decline and current threats to survival are loss and fragmentation of habitat. As a result, this species faces a high risk of extinction from catastrophic events such as floods and drought.

Three Buena Vista Lake shrews were found on the Kern Refuge in 1992 and 1994. Two Buena Vista Lake shrews were live-trapped and released at the capture site in 1998 in the riparian area of Kern Refuge. In 1999, Endangered Species Recovery Program biologists captured and released five Buena Vista Lake shrews at the capture site along a remnant slough in the moist-soil units of Kern Refuge.

In 2000, a limited survey resulted in no captures of Buena Vista Lake shrews on Pixley Refuge on the southern boundary near Deer Creek. Pixley Refuge has little potential habitat for shrews.

Mountain Plover
The mountain plover (*Charadrius montanus*) is a small, killdeer-sized bird. Most mountain plovers winter in California's Central Valley (Sutter and Yuba Counties southward) from September through March. Mountain plovers are also found in foothill valleys west of the San Joaquin Valley, and in the Imperial Valley. This species is a California Species of Concern. The mountain plover is also on the Service's list of Nongame Birds of Conservation Concern for the South Pacific Coast Bird Conservation Region.

Mountain plovers in California winter in plant communities with short vegetation, bare ground, and flat topography such as valley sink scrub, alkali playa, and annual grassland (BLM 1992, Service 1999). Mountain plovers are associated with areas grazed by domestic livestock, giant kangaroo rat precincts, and California ground squirrel colonies. The principle food of mountain plovers are beetles, grasshoppers, crickets, and ants (Service 1999).

The principle threats to mountain plovers are conversion of grassland habitat, agricultural practices in the breeding range, domestic livestock grazing, and decline of native herbivores. Pesticide use in both the wintering and breeding range may also be contributing to the decline of this species.

According to Service records, from 1962 to 1967 mountain plover numbers ranged from 1,000 to 10,000 on Kern Refuge. There have been no recorded sightings of mountain plovers on Kern Refuge since 1985. Mountain plover survey numbers have fluctuated at Pixley Refuge over the years and the Refuge provide habitat for wintering birds although population numbers fluctuate. In a 1993 survey, 109 plovers were counted. In January 1994, 21 birds were counted. The last sighting occurred in January 1997 when 15 birds were observed.

Tricolored Blackbird

The tricolored blackbird (*Agelaius tricolor*) is about the same size as the more common red-winged blackbird and is similar in appearance. The most obvious difference in males is that the bar above the red shoulder patch is white on tricolors instead of yellow. This colonial nesting species is most numerous in California's Central Valley and vicinity. It also occurs less commonly in coastal California, Oregon, and northwestern Baja California (Beedy and Hamilton 1997). The Service classifies the tricolored blackbird as a nongame bird of conservation concern at both the Pacific Region and more local South Pacific Coast Bird Conservation Region scale. The California Department of Fish and Game (CDFG) classifies the tricolored blackbird as a species of special concern.

Tricolored Blackbird. U.S. Fish & Wildlife Service Photo.

Tricolored blackbirds have three requirements for colonial breeding sites: (1) access to open water; (2) a protected nesting substrate (flooded or thorny vegetation); and (3) suitable foraging habitat within about one mile of the nesting colony (Beedy 1989, Beedy and Hamilton 1997). Historically, tricolored blackbird breeding colonies occurred predominately in freshwater marshes dominated by tules and cattails (Beedy and Hamilton 1997). In recent years, an increasing percentage of colonies are in Himalaya blackberries, and silage and grain fields (Beedy and Hamilton 1997).

The primary threats to the tricolored blackbird are predation, inclement weather conditions, habitat loss and alteration, poisoning, contaminants and pollution, and human disturbance (Beedy and Hamilton 1997). At Kern Refuge, the principle cause of nesting failure is predation by black-crowned night herons (J. Allen pers. comm).

Tricolored blackbirds have attempted nesting on Kern Refuge every year since 1992. Increased water supplies for wildlife mandated by recent legislation permits the establishment of nesting habitat in most years. Nesting flocks from 500 to 21,000 birds have been estimated over the years. In the spring of 2000, a colony of approximately 5,000 birds nested on the Refuge. Unfortunately, nesting success was low or nonexistent, presumably due to black-crowned night heron predation, another species that nests in the unit. In 2001, two colonies of tricolored blackbirds nested on Kern Refuge in dense cattails with small amounts of hardstem bulrush. The two colony sizes consisted of approximately 1,000 and 5,000 adult birds and it is believed they had some reproductive success. The larger colony nested next to a colony of nesting white-faced ibis.

Greater Sandhill Crane
Historically, when water is available, lesser and greater sandhill cranes (*Grus canadensis*) roost on the wetlands of Pixley Refuge and feed in the surrounding grazed and agricultural lands. In the winter of 2000/2001, more than 5,000 sandhill cranes were roosting on the Refuge. The shallow water of the Refuge gives roosting cranes protection from ground predators such as coyotes. The subspecies composition is not known but the majority of the birds using the Refuge are lesser sandhill cranes. The greater sandhill crane is listed as a State threatened species.

Vernal Pool Fairy Shrimp
The vernal pool fairy shrimp (*Branchinecta lynchi*) is a small (0.4 to 1-inch long) crustacean with a delicate elongated body, large stalked compound eyes and 11 pairs of swimming legs. This species is endemic to vernal pool habitats in California and southwestern Oregon (Service 1994). The vernal pool fairy shrimp is federally listed as a threatened species.

Vernal pool fairy shrimp typically inhabit vernal pools with clear to tea-colored water, most commonly in grass or mud bottomed swales, or basalt flow depression pools in unplowed grasslands. They also may exist in alkaline vernal pools (Service 1994). The water in pools inhabited by this species has low total dissolved solids (TDS), conductivity, alkalinity, and chloride (Service 1994). Fairy shrimp feed on algae, bacteria, protozoa, rotifers, and bits of detritus (Service 1994).

The primary threats to vernal pool fairy shrimp are the loss and alteration of habitat due to urban and agricultural development and random extinction by virtue of the small isolated nature of many of the remaining populations (Service 1994).

The vernal pools found on the Pixley Refuge are not classic vernal pools but may represent a transition zone from prominent vernal pools further north in the Valley and no pools in the southern end. In 1993, vernal pool fairy shrimp were found in vernal pools on the Two Well Unit (Engler 1993) of Pixley Refuge. The current status of this population is unknown.

White-faced Ibis

White-faced ibis (*Eudocimus albus*) range from northern California, eastern Oregon, southern Idaho, southern Alberta, Canada, Montana, eastern North and South Dakota, and recently northwest Iowa south to the states of Durango and Jalisco in Mexico (Ryder and Manry 1994). Winter range is primarily in coastal Louisana and Texas south to Mexico and Central America. In California, ibis winter in the San Joaquin Valley, at the Salton Sea, and locally in southern California (Rosenberg et al. 1991).

Ibis feed in the shallowly flooded pond margins or mudflats of the Refuges. They fly off the roosting and nesting marshes at Kern Refuge to feed in flood-irrigated agricultural fields. Their diet consists of aquatic and moist-soil invertebrates, especially earthworms and larval insects (mainly Orthoptera, Odonata, Hemiptera, Coleoptera, and Diptera), but also leeches and snails. They may also eat crayfish, small fish, frogs, bivalves, and larvae of chironomid flies (midges) (Ryder and Manry 1994).

White-faced Ibis. Marguerite Gregory © California Academy of Sciences.

White-faced ibis population numbers increased on Kern and Pixley Refuges in the 1990s, mainly due to higher water allocations for the Refuge Complex. Higher water allocations, in times when droughts are not occurring, permit wetlands to be created earlier in the summer as water is delivered to the Refuges and remain longer in the spring as there is more water available to maintain them. White-faced ibis numbers have gone from zero in 1990 to more than 5,600 birds counted on unit 1, the primary roosting area, in June 2001. Also, at least 1,000 ibis active nests were estimated to be in unit 1 in the spring of 2001. Because nesting habitat is limited in the southern Valley, Kern Refuge is important for reproducing birds.

The Pixley Refuge provides important foraging and roosting habitat for the white-faced ibis. In early February 2001, more than 2,200 white-faced ibis were counted at sunset coming into the 300-acre wetland of Pixley Refuge to roost.

Bald Eagle

The bald eagle (*Haliaeetus leucocephalus*) has suffered from habitat destruction and degradation, illegal shooting, and contamination of its food source, most notably due to the pesticide DDT. The bald eagle is listed federally as a threatened species and State listed as an endangered species.

Bald eagles occasionally visit the Kern Refuge during the winter when abundant waterfowl provide a food source. The most recent sighting on the Refuge was in December of 2003.

American Peregrine Falcon

The American peregrine falcon (*Falco peregrinus*) was federally listed as an endangered species in 1970, and State listed as endangered in 1971. In August 1999, the American peregrine falcon was federally delisted.

The American peregrine falcon is seen occasionally on the Kern Refuge especially during the winter when waterfowl populations are high and provide a prey base. Single observations of peregrine falcons have been reported in recent years primarily in the moist-soil units of Kern Refuge in the winter and spring months. Willow trees in the moist-soil units and a few utility poles provide perching sites for the falcons.

Swainson's Hawk.

The Swainson's hawk (*Bueto swainsoni*) is an uncommon breeding resident and migrant in the Central Valley (Polite 2000b). Swainson's hawks breeding in California may spend the winter in Mexico and South America. Central Valley hawks appear to winter in Mexico and Columbia (CDFG 2001). Bloom (1980) estimated 110 nesting pairs, and a total population of 375 pairs in California (Polite 2000b). The Swainson's hawk is State listed as a threatened species.

Declining numbers of Swainson's hawks are caused, in part, from loss of nesting habitat (Polite 2000b). Converting agricultural lands to various residential and commercial developments is a serious threat to Swainson's hawks throughout California (CDFG 2001).

Swainson's hawks are rare migrants at Kern Refuge and reportedly breed further north. There are also records south of Kern Refuge on Kern Waterbank lands. Most sightings for the Refuge occur in July and

August in the riparian area, with occasional sightings in March of a single bird. In mid-August 1993, a prescribed burn on the west side of the Refuge created good foraging habitat and 19 Swainson's hawks were recorded feeding there. One pair of Swainson's hawks did breed in an area north of the Refuge in 1993, and produced three young. Four Swainson's hawks were seen in the Refuge riparian area in 1999, suggesting the Refuge provides limited roosting and foraging habitat as the birds migrate to South America. The birds have not been observed using the Refuge riparian area for nesting sites.

Swainson's hawks have been observed in the vicinity of Kern Refuge in migratory kettles. Kettles of Swainson's hawks have been observed hunting and roosting off Refuge in areas where sheep are grazing, in newly cut alfalfa fields, and in burned areas. The largest kettle of Swainson's hawk's on record contained 95 individuals and was seen in a cut alfalfa field southeast of the Refuge along Wildwood Road in 1994.

Burrowing Owl
At one time, burrowing owls (*Athene cunicularia*) were common and widespread over western North America. However, populations of owls have declined, or disappeared altogether, due to the large scale changes made to the owl's habitat (Souza 1998) including: poisoning and nest site loss resulting from human efforts to control squirrels and prairie dogs (Ehrlich, et. al. 1988); and converting grassland to agriculture (Grinnell and Miller 1944, Zarn 1974, and Remsen 1978). Burrowing owls are listed as a Federal Species of Management Concern and a State Species of Special Concern (Souza 1998).

Kern Refuge provides habitat for burrowing owls in the form of grasslands on the west side along levees that contain abandoned California ground squirrels burrows, and in the entrance tunnels of two artificial kit fox dens. Small grassy areas such as the staging area north of the Refuge's headquarters building, and the mall in front of the headquarters building, may support families of owls in some years. Multiple surveys in the spring and early summer of 1993, yielded counts of 12 distinct burrowing owl locations on Kern Refuge. On one sunrise survey conducted in July 1999, on the east side of Goose Lake Canal on Kern Refuge, five burrowing owls were counted. On night survey on the Kern Refuge conducted along a 12.1-mile route on the west side of Goose Lake Canal, five burrowing owls were counted in June of 1998.

Pixley Refuge, consisting of primarily grazed grasslands, provides more habitat for burrowing owls. Multiple surveys conducted on Pixley Refuge in the spring and early summer of 1993, yielded 20 burrowing owl sites on Pixley Main (consisting of the Wetland, Centerfield, Two-Well, Deer Creek West and Deer Creek East Units) and the Dickey Tract. In addition, during this season, six burrowing owl locations were recorded on Pixley's Horse Pasture Unit.

On a sunrise survey of Pixley Main conducted on July 6, 1999, 48 burrowing owls were observed. On a sunrise survey of the Horse Pasture Unit, conducted July 8, 1999, 28 burrowing owls were counted.

Later that morning, 45 burrowing owls were counted at the Los Feliz Unit. On a 15.2-mile night survey route on Pixley Main, ten burrowing owls were counted in June 2001. Four burrowing owls were counted on the same survey route on a night survey in July 2001.

Lost Hills Saltbush

Lost Hills saltbush is an annual that flowers from May to August (Service 1998). It reaches a maximum height of eight inches (Service 1998). The male and female flowers are mixed in small clusters in the upper leaf axils. The fruiting bracts are broadly triangular, irregularly toothed, and may or may not have tubercles. Lost Hills saltbush is listed as a Federal species of concern. It is one of the plant species included in the Recovery Plan for Upland Species of the San Joaquin Valley, California (Service 1998).

This species exists in the Valley sink scrub, Valley saltbush scrub, nonnative grassland, and alkali meadow plant communities (Service 1998). At most sites, Lost Hills saltbush grows in dried beds of alkaline pools; however, one population, south of McKittrick, exists on exposed slopes rich in gypsum (Service 1998). Associated species include common saltbush, spiny saltbush, alkali heath, saltgrass, and seepweed (Service 1998). Valley-floor populations exist at elevations of 165 to 280 feet (Service 1998).

Prior to 1980, Lost Hills saltbush was reported in three general areas: north of Lost Hills; Mendota in Fresno County; and the Carrizo Plain in San Luis Obispo County (Service 1998). In the 1980s, a number of additional sites were discovered, and the species was confirmed to exist near Lost Hills and on the Carrizo Plain (Service 1998). The Lost Hills and Carrizo Plain sites represented large (greater than 10,000 plants) metapopulations, but most sites had a few hundred individuals or less in 1993 (Service 1998).

Lost Hills saltbush has been eliminated in some areas by converting land to agricultural use (Service 1998). Threats to this species include degraded habitat by livestock grazing, commercial and agricultural development, flooding for waterfowl management, and off-road vehicle activity (Service 1998).

Although Lost Hills saltbush has not been the subject of direct conservation efforts, it has benefitted indirectly from acquisitions directed at other species (Service 1998). The most important task for conservation of Lost Hills saltbush is to protect existing populations on private land from ongoing threats (Service 1998). To do so, sites must be secured through conservation easements or acquisition, and public agencies must agree to protect habitat on public lands (Service 1998).

In May 1991, a cursory survey was conducted of the San Joaquin Desert Research Natural Area (RNA), located in the northwest corner of the Kern Refuge, by the now late Jack Zaninovich, of the California Native Plant Society, and the Refuge biologist (Service 1991). Lost Hills saltbush was located and identified by Mr. Zaninovich in unit 12, which is within the RNA (Service 1991). This was the first record of this species for the Refuge (Service 1991). The heavy March rains resulted in a lush growth of many native forbs and probably increased the numbers of this small population of Lost Hills saltbush to a detectable level (Service 1991). Surveys by botanists skilled enough to identify various species of Atriplex have not been conducted in the RNA since 1991.

Diseases and Toxins

When wildlife is exposed to bacterial, fungal, viral, or parasitic diseases, or chemical and biotoxins, the results can be massive die-offs of migratory waterfowl and it can be detrimental to resident wildlife populations. Suitable conditions for the outbreak and spread of diseases could occur on the Refuges because of infected migratory waterfowl, shorebirds, and neotropical migrants using the Refuge. Exposure to toxins could occur on the Refuges or on surrounding agricultural land. While relatively little is known about the general health of most wildlife, sufficient data exists on the Refuge's to minimize, and if necessary, prevent major outbreaks and exposures of waterfowl and waterbirds to at least some chemicals and biotoxins. Management of other diseases has not been evaluated on the Refuges, but a network of qualified agencies and organizations would provide support for control and containment. Summarized below are real and potential toxin issues on the Refuges.

Chemical Toxins

Chemical toxin exposure on the Refuges could occur directly through lead shot, indirectly through rodenticides, and indirectly or directly through insecticides and herbicides.

Lead Shot. Lead shot was commonly used for waterfowl hunting until 1991, when the Service banned its use. Since 1991, steel shot has been used to hunt waterfowl. Infrequently, other nontoxic shot such as bismuth and tungsten are also used. In 1976, as part of a region-wide effort to address lead toxicity in waterfowl, 115 soil samples were taken that represented approximately 10 percent of the Kern Refuge wetland area. The number of lead pellets averaged 68,300 per acre and ranged from 8,094 to 147,155 pellets per acre. The range was reflective of the number of years a wetland unit had been exposed to hunting. Unit 1 had the highest average because it has been hunted 13 years and unit 6C had the lowest average because it has been hunted only 1 year. Also, as part of a related region-wide effort to address lead toxicity in waterfowl, gizzard samples were obtained from harvested waterfowl during the 1975 to 1976, 1981 to 1982, and 1984 to 1985 hunt seasons. A total of 628 gizzards, mostly from pintails (78 percent), were examined for ingested lead pellets. The overall ingestion rate decreased from 8 percent in 1975 to 1976 to 2.7 percent in 1981 to 1982, to 2.2 percent in 1984 to 1985. At the time of these studies, the results were more indicative of pintails than any other species examined (mallard, shoveler, green-winged teal) and probably did not accurately reflect the lead pellet ingestion rate by waterfowl on the Kern Refuge.

Since lead shot has been banned on the Refuge for more than 10 years, and because wetlands are periodically maintained through discing and plowing, lead poisoning is no longer the threat it once was. Periodic maintenance of wetland soils may aid in any remnant lead pellets migrating further into the soil, so that they will not be available to waterfowl when wetlands are flooded.

Rodenticides. Rodenticides are not used on the Refuge. They may be used on surrounding land, which could result in secondary exposure to either transient or resident wildlife on the Refuge.

Insecticides. The use of insecticides on the Refuge is governed by approved Pesticide Use Proposals and Compatibility Determinations. Limited use occurs to control mosquitoes to reduce the likelihood of serious public health risks, especially Encephalitis. The Kern County Mosquito Abatement District applies methoprene (a growth inhibitor) and BTI (biological control) in selected wetland areas only after field surveys document high mosquito densities. Published studies have documented that exposure of resident and migratory land-based and wetland wildlife to these larvacides causes little or no adverse effect to species or population persistence and longevity.

Herbicides. The use of herbicides on the Refuge is governed by approved Pesticide Use Proposals and Compatibility Determinations. Both Rodeo and Roundup are used seasonally to control vegetation, especially cattails, around water control structures and in ditches and canals, and Garlon is used occasionally to control salt cedar.

Diseases

A Waterfowl Disease Plan, written in 1976, and a Disease Contingency Plan, written in 1984, provide a history and summary of disease outbreaks on the Refuges and surrounding lands from 1960 to 1983. These plans identify water level manipulation, habitat management, and planning as key elements in preventing, controlling, and managing waterfowl diseases. A Service Migratory Bird Disease Contingency Plan (1984) provides a framework for coordinating disease control and prevention.

The most serious disease on the Refuges is avian botulism and to a lesser extent avian cholera. For both of these, the Refuges could serve as a primary or secondary outbreak source. Avian botulism was first documented on Pixley Refuge in 1963, and in 1967 on Kern Refuge. Stagnant and poorly circulated water were identified as the causes in both initial outbreaks. Since that time, avian botulism has periodically been diagnosed on the Kern Refuge but infrequently on the Pixley Refuge. Water management (most wetlands are dry in June and July) has played a key role in reducing the likelihood of outbreaks on the Refuges, but the risk of birds becoming infected elsewhere and then using the Refuges, remains the same.

Avian cholera was suspected in the death of one Canada goose on the Kern Refuge in 1968, and confirmed in the death of 96 birds in 1984. No outbreaks of or documented waterfowl deaths due to avian cholera have occurred on either of the Refuges since then, however, its occurrence in the Pacific Flyway is well documented.

Cultural Resources

Cultural Resources Defined

Cultural resources are physical remains, sites, objects, records, oral testimonies, and traditions that connect us to our nation's past. Cultural resources include archaeological and historical artifacts, sites, landscapes, plants, animals, sacred locations, and traditional cultural properties that play an important role in the traditional, but continuing, life of a community. Most of the recorded cultural resources at the Refuges are archaeological sites.

Cultural resources, especially archaeological sites, are fragile and nonrenewable. Most consist of worked stone, fire altered rocks, and organically enriched soil on, or close to, the surface. When compared to the surrounding landscape and contemporary cultural features, such as roads, ditches, and structures, archaeological sites are small and subtle.

Prehistoric Setting

At various times the shore of Pleistocene era Lake Tulare would have been within what is now the Refuge. No archaeological evidence clearly demonstrates a Pleistocene human presence within the Refuge, however, discoveries nearby of fluted points, similar to the well known Clovis style projectile point, provide a hint of a human occupation around Lake Tulare for more than 9,000 years (Riddel and Olsen 1969, Preston 1981).

The Refuge is situated on two historic slough channels that fed the Holocene Lake Tulare before it was drained for agricultural production. Marshes, sloughs, and lakes often provide rich resources for sustaining human life. The 1983 overview of cultural resources of the Refuge predicted that most sites are located above 218 feet mean sea level at the contact between Twissleman and Nahrub soil types (Arguelles 1983). These may represent the uplands and slough channels as they existed during the early Holocene Period. Many archaeological sites are found at bends in former sloughs and on large islands internal to the marsh.

Ethnographic Setting

When Europeans first came to California, the Yokuts inhabited most of the Valley. Settlement by people culturally akin to the Yokuts probably began about 7,000 years ago (Preston 1981). Their artifacts were much like those of Great Basin peoples but showed adjustments to a more westerly environment (Preston 1981). Latta (1949) estimated that before the coming of Europeans to California, the Yokuts numbered no less than 25,000 living in and around the Tulare Basin. In 1833, an epidemic, possibly a severe strain of malaria, wiped out 75 percent of the native population (Wallace 1978).

Historic Setting

Spanish Period. Pedro Fages left the first written record of the southern Valley. As acting governor of Alta California in the fall of 1772,

Fages led a small band of soldiers through Tejon Pass and down into the Valley (Fages 1937). He visited the Yokut village of Tulamniu, which he named Buena Vista (Wallace 1978). From that time until 1806, except for a few vague reports of expeditions searching for deserting soldiers and mission runaways, there is no record of the Spanish visiting the southern Valley.

In 1806, Father Jose Maria de Zalvidea and Alferez Gabriel Moraga accompanied Lieutenant Francis Ruiz from Mission Santa Barbara via Mission Santa Ynez into the Valley from the west, traversing, as Fages had done three decades earlier, around Buena Vista Lake and through what is now southern Kern County. Because the rest of California was rich and underpopulated, the Spanish saw little value in the Tulare Basin.

Mexican Period. While Spanish authorities in California viewed the southern Valley with disinterest, the Mexicans saw it as a threat to their authority. It was a refuge and staging area for increasingly aggressive Yokuts raids and a route for illegal trappers, explorers, and settlers from the United States (U.S.).

When California became part of Mexico (1822-1846), expeditions into the Valley were largely punitive. Ranchers organized campaigns to recover stolen livestock, punish thieves, and capture slaves.

During the winter of 1826 to 1827, Jedediah Smith, the first U.S. citizen to enter the Valley, started trapping in the basin. His stories and the quality of the pelts he brought back encouraged the Hudson Bay Company to send trappers into California. Between 1832 and 1845 the Southern Trapping Party of the Hudson Bay Company employed 90 to 100 men in the Valley (Elliott 1883).

John C. Fremont explored the Valley in 1844 and 1845 (Preston 1981). In 1846, Fremont named the river the Spanish called Rio de San Felipe and La Porcincula, after his cartographer Edward M. Kern.

U.S. Settlement. Although Tulare Basin did not experience an invasion by the first wave of immigrants, gold seekers and settlers soon overran the country and Indian lands passed into private hands. In 1851, the tribes agreed to relinquish their lands for reservations and payments in goods, but the treaty was never ratified by the U. S. Senate (Wallace 1978).

The key to agriculture in the Valley is irrigation. The first irrigation ditch in the basin was built between 1862 and 1867 (Preston 1981). Lake Tulare's water levels fell and annual hydrologic cycles were disrupted as water was drawn from the Tulare Basin for irrigation. Natural stream courses were channelized and marshlands were drained for agricultural purposes. In 1898, articles in the Hanford Daily Journal and the Tulare County Times reported that the lake had dried up.

Soils were an important factor in historic land use as they determined areas suitable for cultivation and grazing. Many soils initially favorable to historic agricultural methods were soon abandoned due to the accumulations of salts resulting from irrigation. Other soils, Pond Loam, Fresno clay, and to a lesser extent Nahrub clay were so heavy or compact that they would not yield to the plow, but did produce vegetation suitable for grazing (Arguelles 1983).

As Tulare County's reputation as grazing land grew, cattlemen streamed into the southern section. By the 1860s, the Visalia region had 3,300 non-Indian residents. Overgrazing and poor land management practices took their toll on the land and the people who settled there (Preston 1981).

When the first rail line extended into the Tulare Basin in 1871, many of the cattle ranchers sold out and wheat and sheep farms spread across the basin. Between 1870 and 1880, Tulare County's population increased 149 percent from 4,533 to 11,281. By 1890 it had risen to 24,574, an additional 118 percent.

Surveys

Most archaeological surveys in areas of Kern and Pixley Refuges have been done in conjunction with Federal projects. About 20 percent (2,102 acres) of Kern Refuge's 10,618 acres have been systematically surveyed for cultural resources. The remaining acreage includes about 33 percent (3,500 acres) managed as wetland and about 14 percent (1,500 acres) that was previously leveled agricultural fields, neither of which are likely to have intact archaeological sites. About 6 percent (387 acres) of Pixley Refuge's 6,379 acres have been systematically surveyed for cultural resources.

Paleontological Resources

Kern Refuge. Vertebrate fossils including a presumed mammoth (Arguelles 1983) and camelid remains (Grayson 1985) have been located within the Kern Refuge boundary. Beyond identification, no formal study of these fossils has been undertaken. No significant fossil finds would be expected within the Refuge. However, their discovery is a possibility. If collected, paleontological resources should be managed under the Department of the Interior's Museum Property program.

Pixley Refuge. No significant fossil finds have been found, within the Pixley Refuge boundary. Discovery is, however, a possibility.

Prehistoric Resources

Kern Refuge. There are 26 recorded prehistoric sites within the Kern Refuge boundary, including burial areas, camp sites, and lithic scatter. A formal evaluation for eligibility to the National Register of Historic Places (NRHP) was started for the Poso Creek archaeological site, a prehistoric burial area. The nomination was returned by the National Park Service due to insufficient data. No further efforts have been taken to list this site on the NRHP. Eight prehistoric sites have been evaluated and determined not eligible for listing. Until listed or evaluated as ineligible all other sites should be treated as eligible for listing on the NRHP. It is probable that over the coming years archaeological sites may be inadvertently exposed by natural or human actions.

Several sites are currently mapped closely together. Additional survey data may show these to be a single site or an associated cluster. Given the area's fluctuating hydrology, some sites may be deeply buried. Discovery of these sites through standard surface survey is unlikely.

Pixley Refuge. There are three recorded prehistoric sites on Pixley Refuge. All consist of lithic scatter. In addition, one isolated prehistoric artifact (basal projectile point fragment) has been found on the Refuge. One prehistoric site lies just to the west of the Refuge. Three of the largest sites appear to have been dislocated from their original context and incorporated into levees. No sites have been formally evaluated for eligibility for listing on the NRHP. Until listed or evaluated as not eligible, all sites will be treated as eligible for listing on the NRHP. It is probable that over the coming years archaeological sites may be inadvertently exposed by natural or human actions.

Historic Resources
Kern Refuge. Two historic sites were recorded on Kern Refuge. Both consist of domestic debris from the first quarter of the twentieth century, such as cans that once held milk and tobacco, bottles, canning jars, and various metal objects. In 1983, these sites were determined not eligible for listing on the NRHP. Because the area was deemed swamp land during early surveys and not suitable for agriculture, physical remains of historic sites are likely to be few in number and primarily reflective of ranching activities.

Pixley Refuge. Three historic sites have been recorded on the Pixley Refuge. They are composed largely of brick and some glass. The items date to the last quarter of the nineteenth century and the first quarter of the twentieth century. They likely correspond with the 1890s homesteads of M.P. Traniar and J. Armstrong (Arguelles 1983).

Visitor Services
The wetlands at Kern Refuge provide numerous opportunities for outdoor recreation including hunting, wildlife observation, photography, and environmental education. Over the past three years, Kern Refuge has averaged about 6,000 visitors annually. Until recently, the only visitor services on Pixley Refuge were guided public talks and tours. Pixley Refuge has averaged about 230 visitors per year over the last three years. Figure 10 shows the existing visitor facilities on Kern Refuge.

Refuge Access
Kern Refuge's entrance is located at the intersection of Garces Highway and Corcoran Road. The entrance is about 14 miles from Interstate 5 via State Highway 46 and Corcoran Road and 19 miles west of State Highway 99 via Garces Highway. Kern Refuge has a small paved parking lot at the headquarters with space for about eight vehicles and a larger gravel parking lot at the nearby hunter check station with space

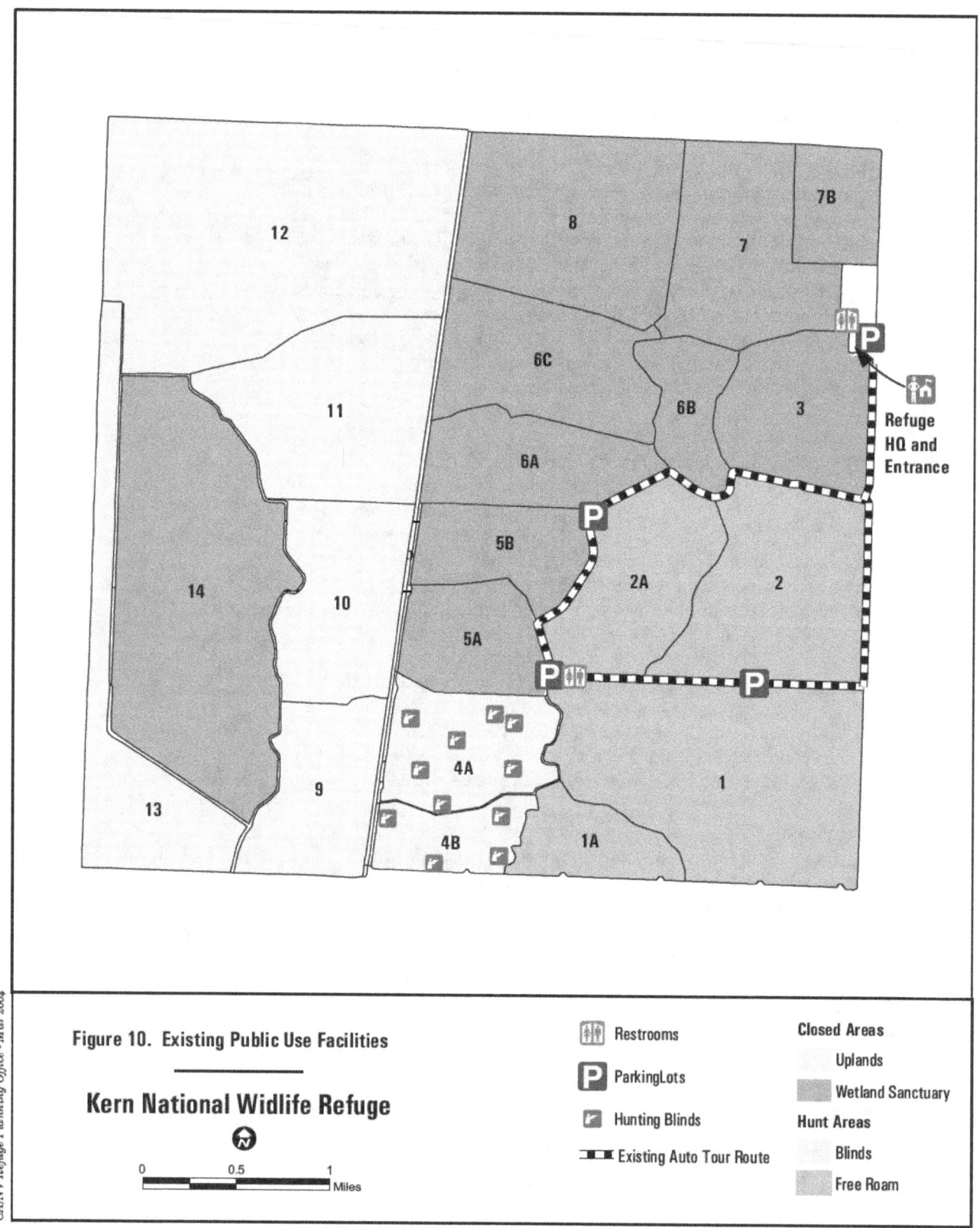

Figure 10. Existing Public Use Facilities

Kern National Widlife Refuge

0   0.5   1
Miles

Restrooms

P ParkingLots

Hunting Blinds

Existing Auto Tour Route

Closed Areas

Uplands

Wetland Sanctuary

Hunt Areas

Blinds

Free Roam

Refuge HQ and Entrance

for up to 75 vehicles. Three gravel parking lots with space for 20 to 30 vehicles each, are located along the five-mile gravel auto tour route. In addition to vehicles, the tour route is also open to bicycles and pedestrians.

Pixley Refuge is located about 6.7 miles from Highway 99 via Avenue 56 and Road 88. The entrance to Pixley Refuge's parking lot is located off Road 88, about one mile north of Avenue 56. The gravel parking lot has space for about 12 vehicles.

Hunting

Waterfowl hunting has occurred on Kern Refuge since the early 1960s and is administered by CDFG through a cooperative agreement. Kern Refuge is the only public hunt area in the southern Valley. An average of 1,800 visitors per year hunt on the Refuge. From 1995 to 2002, the number of hunters at Kern Refuge has more than doubled from 1,236 to 2,830. Hunters account for about 39 percent of the Refuge's visitors. Currently, Kern Refuge has 11 hunting blinds spaced across 479 acres. Two of the blinds are wheelchair-accessible. A maximum of four hunters are allowed per blind. Kern Refuge also provides up to 1,867 acres of free roam hunt area. The maximum hunter density in this area is one hunter per 20 acres, for a total capacity of 93 hunters. The amount of the Refuge open to hunting depends on the acreage of flooded wetland habitat. The first 1,000 acres of the Refuge's wetlands flooded, are closed to hunting. As the remaining wetland acreage is flooded, 55 percent is closed to hunting and 45 percent is opened. During drought years, hunting may be completely closed or only open on a small area of the Refuge. Thus, the size of the hunt area is related to the availability of water.

The duck-hunting season generally runs from late October or early November to mid-January. At Kern Refuge, hunt days are Wednesdays and Saturdays from a half hour before sunrise to sunset. Hunter success at Kern Refuge is consistently higher than the State average. Over a 7-year period from 1995 to 2002, hunters at Kern Refuge averaged 2.7 ducks per visit while, the State average over the same period was 1.7 ducks per hunter visit. Figure 11 illustrates this trend.

Hunters travel from all over California to hunt at Kern Refuge. However, most hunters are from two general areas: the southern Valley (Kern, Tulare, and Kings Counties) and the Los Angeles Basin (Los Angeles, Ventura, and Orange Counties). While about 34 percent of hunters traveled less than 50 miles to hunt on the Kern Refuge, 51 percent traveled more than 100 miles to hunt the Refuge during the 1999 hunt season.

Figure 11. Average Duck Harvest per Hunter Visit: 1995 to 2002.

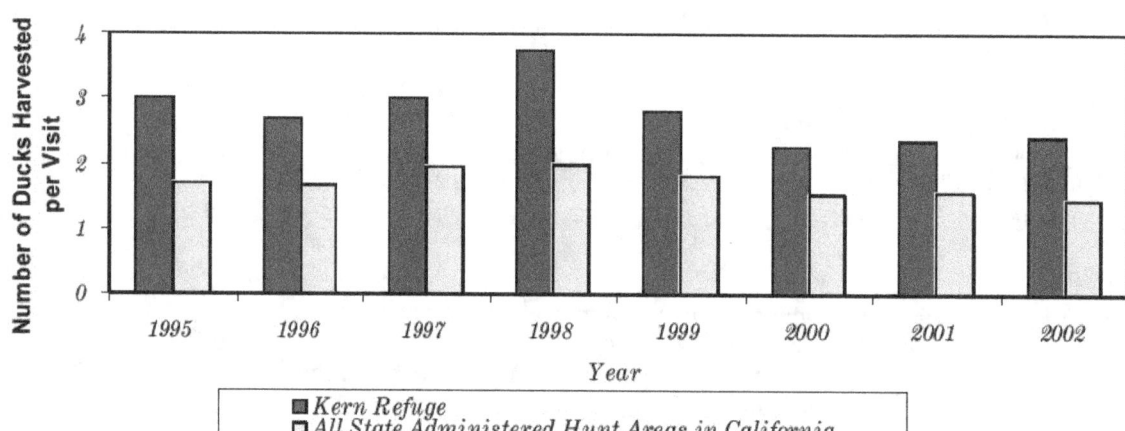

Hunting is not permitted on Pixley Refuge for a number of reasons. First, the Refuge is an important wintering area for sandhill cranes and the wetland area is too small to provide adequate sanctuary for the cranes and allow hunting. Second, due to the small size of the wetland unit, relatively few hunters could be safely accommodated. Furthermore, a hunt program would be difficult to administer due to the lack of staff present on the Refuge. Finally, as a wildlife sanctuary, Pixley Refuge's wetlands attract waterfowl to the area, including nearby private wetlands that are hunted.

Wildlife Observation, Interpretation and Environmental Education
About 1,500 visitors participate in wildlife observation and 2,000 visitors participate in interpretation activities on Kern Refuge each year. The Refuge offers wildlife observation and photography opportunities along a five-mile self-guided auto tour route. Foot access is also allowed on established dike roads. The auto tour route is open year-round during daylight hours, except during the waterfowl hunting season. During this period, the Refuge is closed to the nonhunting public on hunt days (Wednesdays and Saturdays). During the peak waterfowl migration, and wintering period (September 15 through February 15), visitor services are limited to the self-guided auto tour route, until 1,000 acres of wetlands are flooded. Once this initial sanctuary is established, 45 percent of the remaining wetland units are opened to foot travel as they are flooded.

Over the last three years, an average of about 445 visitors per year participate in staff or volunteer conducted talks, tours, and demonstrations at Kern Refuge. Approximately 340 students per year participate in Refuge-related environmental education, conducted by Refuge staff or volunteers either on or off Refuge.

In 2000, Pixley Refuge staff and Tulare County Audubon Society volunteers constructed a parking lot and a 1.5-mile interpretive walking trail and observation platform on the wetland unit at the Refuge. The trail guides visitors through 13 interpretive stops as well as six interpretive panels ending at an observation platform overlooking the east end of the managed wetland unit. The majority of the use occurs on the trail from fall to spring coinciding with bird migrations and waterfowl and waterbird use of the wetland habitat. Little use is expected in the summer months when the wetlands are dry.

Socioeconomics

Economic Region

Location. Kern Refuge is in the southern end of the Valley in the Tulare Basin, 19 miles west of Delano, California, in Kern County. Kern County is in the heart of Central California with an economic base of agriculture and oil. The Kern County land area is 2,000 square miles making it the third largest county in California. Kern Refuge, a single 10,618-acre unit, is surrounded by privately owned pasture (nonnative grassland), native scrublands, and agricultural croplands.

Pixley Refuge is approximately 19 miles south of Tulare and 15 miles northwest of Kern Refuge, in Tulare County. Tulare County is about midway between San Francisco and Los Angeles. Tulare County consists of 2,000 square miles. The eastern half of the county (52 percent) (U.S. Census Bureau 2003, California Research Bureau 1997) is primarily public land. These public lands include Kings Canyon National Park, Sequoia National Park, Sequoia National Forest, and Inyo National Forest.

Population

As of January 2001, Kern County's population was 685,800 (about 2 percent of the State's population). Bakersfield, about 110 miles north of Los Angeles, is the County seat and the largest city in Kern County with a population of 254,400. Delano, Wasco, and Lost Hills, the cities nearest Kern Refuge, have populations of 38,824, 20,092, and 2,212, respectively. The combined population of the unincorporated portions of the County is 276,200. The 2000 population for Census Tract 45, in which Kern Refuge is located, was 3,418, of this, 88 percent were Hispanic, 10 percent were white, 0.5 percent were black, 0.5 percent were American Indian, Eskimo, or Aleut, and 1 percent were Asian or Pacific Islander (U.S. Census Bureau 2003).

The population of Tulare County, as of January 2001, was 375,550 (1.1 percent of the State's population). Of all the California counties, Tulare County is ranked first in agricultural production. Tulare County is also the second largest agricultural producing area in the United States and the number one milk producer in the world (California Department of Food and Agriculture 2002). Visalia, the County seat, is the largest city with a population of 94,300. Other major cities include Tulare, population 41,000, and Porterville, population 40,650. The combined population of the unincorporated portions of the County is 144,300. The 2000 population of Census Tract 43, which includes the Pixley Refuge, was 6,746, of this 80 percent were Hispanic, 13 percent were White, 4 percent were Asian or Pacific Islander, 1 percent were Black, 1 percent were American Indian, Eskimo, or Aleut, and 1 percent were other (U.S. Census Bureau 2003).

Employment

The civilian workforce in Kern County for 2000 was 287,000 (1.09 percent of the State's population). The average per-capita income in 1999 was $19,886. The unemployment rate was 11.3 percent. In Tract 45, the 2000 workforce of persons 16 and older was 2,188, of those, 22 percent were unemployed. Median household income for Tract 45 in 2000 was $30,547. In Tract 45, 39 percent of the population lives below the poverty level, of those, 35 percent are under 18 and 24 percent are 65 and older (U.S. Census Bureau 2003).

In Kern County, the agriculture industry employed 46,900 people. Agriculture sales for the County in 2000 totaled $2.2 billion; this is 7.5 percent of the State's total agricultural income. Leading commodities in the County are grapes, citrus, almonds and by-products, cotton and processed cottonseed, milk, carrots, pistachios, cattle and calves, hay, and alfalfa. Of these commodities, California retains only 2 percent of the crops with approximately 18 percent exported to other nations and 80 percent shipped to other states. In 2000, Kern County was the fourth most productive agricultural county in the State.

The 2000 civilian labor force in Tulare County was 143,800, about 0.7 percent of the State's total. The average per-capita income in 1997 was $17,116. The 2000 work force in Census Tract 43, of persons 16 and older, was 3,172; of those, 1,394 were unemployed. Median household income is $19,185. In 2000, 38 percent of the population of Tract 43 lived in poverty; of those, 48 percent were 18 and younger and 13 percent were 65 and older (U.S. Census Bureau 2003).

In 1999, 34,900 people in Tulare County were employed in the agricultural industry. The value of agricultural production in Tulare County for 1998 was $2.9 billion. This represents 10.8 percent of California's total agricultural production. Leading commodities were livestock and livestock products, poultry and poultry products, field crops, vegetables, fruits and nuts, nursery products, seed crops, apiary products, milk, oranges, grapes, cattle and calves, hay and silage, alfalfa, plums, corn, grain and silage, nectarines, peaches, and cotton.

Refuge Economics

In 1996, 77 million people in the United States, 16 and older, participated in hunting, fishing, and wildlife watching; this is more than the total attendance in 1996 for all major league baseball and football games, which was 73.8 million. Of the 77 million wildlife enthusiasts, 62 million, almost one-third of the population of the United States, were wildlife watchers, this does not include hunting or visits to zoos, aquariums, or circuses. Americans spent $29.2 billion to observe, feed, and photograph wildlife in the United States, according to the 1996 National and State Economic Impacts of Wildlife Watching report (Service 1998, Claudill and Laughland 1998). According to the report, more than one million jobs are created by wildlife watching, which generates $24.2 billion in employment income, $323.5 million in state income tax revenue, and $3.8 billion in Federal income tax revenue. Wildlife watching also produces $1.04 billion in state sales tax revenue. Since 1991, wildlife watchers have increased by 21 percent (Service 1998, Claudill and Laughland 1998). If wildlife watching had been a Fortune 500 company in 1996, it would have ranked 23rd (Claudill and Laughland 1998, Service 1998).

In 1995, visitors to National Wildlife Refuges across the country contributed more than $401.1 million in sales to regional economies. As this spending flowed through the economy, more than 10,000 people were employed generating $162.9 million in employment income (Claudill and Laughland 1998). In 1996, wildlife watchers in California spent $2.1 billion and created 47,716 jobs that generated $1.1 million in income. This in turn resulted in $127.4 million in state sales tax revenue, $45.1 million in state income tax revenue, and $178.6 million in Federal income tax revenue (Claudill and Laughland 1998).

In Kern County, travelers spent $788.8 million in 1998. The tourism industry employed 9,340 workers for a payroll of $121.4 million. County and State tax revenue generated by tourism totaled $13.2 million and $43 million respectively.

Millions of tourists travel through Tulare County each year to visit Sequoia National Park and Kings Canyon National Park. In 1998, travelers spent $425.4 million in Tulare County. The tourism industry employed 4,860 workers for a payroll of $64.2 million, which generated $7.1 million in local taxes and $23.1 million in State taxes.

In fiscal year 2000, Refuge Revenue Sharing programs contributed $23,091 to Kern County and $9,325 to Tulare County. Grazing Receipts for Pixley Refuge were $18,756. On Kern Refuge, grazing receipts of $8,210 were used for habitat improvement projects. The two Refuges spent $498,400 for local contracts and another $160,000 was spent locally for goods and services. Salaries for Refuge employees, who live locally, totaled $530,000.

Chapter 4. Problems and Opportunities

Historic Habitat Destruction and Modification

Kern Refuge was created in 1960 to replace wetland habitat in the southern San Joaquin Valley (Valley) lost as a result of draining and converting wetlands for agricultural use. Prior to the increase in agriculture, at least two streams that originated in the Sierra Nevada Mountains 40 to 60 miles to the east, meandered near the present day Refuge and ultimately emptied into Tulare Lake. Occasionally, during years of higher than average rainfall, these streams would overflow and flood major areas of the relatively flat Valley floor, including the area now occupied by the Refuge. These naturally flowing streams, occasional flooding, and relatively little agriculture resulted in a connected system of riparian corridors, wetland vegetation, and seasonal wetlands in the Valley. These natural processes and features are no longer apparent in the Valley, which today represents a landscape that has been drastically modified to meet agricultural demands. The Refuge, like the surrounding landscape, is also highly modified, with a series of constructed water delivery canals and ditches, water control structures, and regularly-shaped wetland units bounded by levees.

Pixley Refuge was created in 1959 to replace wetlands lost due to draining by early settlers. Parts of Pixley Refuge are within the historic Tulare Lake Bed that once provided significant habitat for waterfowl on the Pacific Flyway. Draining the Tulare Lake Bed destroyed traditional habitat for migratory waterfowl. Other agricultural alterations in the southern San Joaquin Valley diminished upland habitat for native species as well. The Pixley Refuge preserves a portion of native upland habitat, which was once common on the lower portions of the Tulare Basin. Most of the other native uplands have been destroyed due to agriculture, urban development, and overgrazing. Today, only in high runoff years do flood flows reach the Tulare Lake Basin. In normal years, flows are retained in specific flood control areas for farming. The Tulare Basin watershed now has numerous reservoirs that hold the water to generate power, control flooding, and irrigate throughout the season. Continuing development around the Refuge could potentially become a problem, as dairies and other types of agriculture eliminate native habitat.

Nonnative Plant Species

Nonnative plant species, especially salt cedar, continue to be problematic along levees and in wetland units. Although salt cedar provides habitat for some wildlife, most researchers have concluded that it has little value to most native amphibians, reptiles, birds, and mammals (Lovich and de Gouvenain 1998). While labor-intensive management (cutting it to a stump and painting the stump with herbicide) is effective in controlling salt cedar, treating large areas is expensive and the Refuge lacks the staff to implement this control method. Biological control is feasible but still uncertain, mechanical removal is site limited, and the use of foliar herbicides is being investigated. An integrated approach is being used

Chapter 6. Plan Implementation

Once the preferred management alternative has been finalized, the CCP has been approved, and the Service has notified the public of its decision, the implementation phase of the CCP process begins. During the next 15 years, the objectives and strategies presented in this CCP would be realized; the CCP would serve as the primary reference document for all Refuge Complex planning, operations, and management until it is formally revised. The Service would implement the final CCP with assistance from existing and new partner agencies and organizations and the public.

Activities needed to realize the management strategies discussed in this CCP are referred to as projects. Every effort would be made to implement these projects by the deadlines established here. However, the timing of implementation of the management activities proposed in this document is contingent upon a variety of factors, including:

- Funding,
- Staffing,
- Completion of detailed step-down management plans,
- Compliance with other Federal laws and regulations,
- Partnerships, and
- The results of monitoring and evaluation.

Each of these factors is described briefly below as it applies to the Service's proposed action.

Funding and Staffing

To implement the proposed action and to achieve the objectives and goals of this CCP, the Service would need additional funding and staff. Appendix E describes the budget proposals and staffing needs for Kern and Pixley Refuges, respectively, for each project proposed in this CCP. Full implementation of all of the projects proposed in this CCP would require the Service to increase Kern Refuge Complex's current annual operations budget by 43 percent to approximately $820,000.

If the proposed action is implemented, full staffing for both Kern and Pixley Refuges would include the following positions.
- Project leader
- Deputy project leader
- Wildlife biologist
- Private lands biologist
- Administrative support assistant
- Office automation clerk
- Refuge operations specialist
- Three engineering equipment operators
- Maintenance worker
- Outdoor recreation planner
- Law Enforcement Officer
- Biological Science Technician

Step-Down Management Plans

Some projects or types of projects require more in-depth planning than the CCP process is designed to provide. For these projects, the Service prepares step-down management plans. In essence, step-down management plans provide the additional planning details necessary to implement management strategies identified in a CCP. Kern and Pixley Refuges currently have a number of step-down plans already completed. These include plans for fire management (Appendix K), disease prevention and control, and pest management. This CCP proposes several new step-down plans that are identified in Table 1 along with their target date for completion.

Table 1. Proposed New Step-Down Plans.

Step Down Plans	Target Year for Completion
Land Protection Plan – Wetlands	2005
Comprehensive Inventory and Monitoring Plan	2006
Grassland Management Plan	2006
Visitor Services Plan	2007
Land Protection Plan – Upland Linkages and Threatened and Endangered Species Habitat[2]	2008
Poso Creek Flood Water Management Plan	2016

Compliance Requirements

This CCP was developed to comply with all Federal laws, executive orders, and legislative acts to the extent possible. Some activities (particularly those that involve revising an existing step-down management plan or preparing a new one) would need to comply with other laws or regulations. In addition to NEPA and the Improvement Act, full implementation of all components of this CCP would require compliance with:

- Executive Order 11988 (Floodplain Management);
- Executive Order 12372 (Intergovernmental Review of Federal Programs);
- Executive Order 11593 (Protection of Historical, Archaeological, and Scientific Properties);
- Executive Order 11990 (Protection of Wetlands);
- Executive Order 12996 (Management and General Public Use of the National Wildlife Refuge System);
- Executive Order 12898 (Environmental Justice in Minority Populations and Low-Income Populations);
- Secretarial Order 3127 (Hazardous Substances Determinations);
- Endangered Species Act of 1973, as amended;
- Refuge Recreation Act of 1962, as amended; and the
- National Historic Preservation Act of 1966, as amended.

---

[2] Subject to the approval of the Director of the Fish and Wildlife Service

Partnership Opportunities

As described in Chapter 1, a number of partners play an important role in helping the Service achieve its goals and objectives for Kern and Pixley Refuges. The Service would continue to rely on these and other partners in the future to help implement this CCP and to provide input for future CCP updates. This CCP identifies many projects that provide new opportunities for existing or new partners. There is great potential for more public participation and assistance in the management and interpretation of the Refuges. The Service welcomes and encourages more public participation in the Refuges.

Adaptive Management

This CCP provides for adaptive management of Kern and Pixley Refuges. Adaptive management is a flexible approach to long-term management of biotic resources that is directed by the results of ongoing monitoring activities and new data. Management techniques, objectives, and strategies are regularly evaluated in light of monitoring results, new scientific understanding, and other new information. These periodic evaluations are used to adapt management objectives and techniques to better achieve the Refuge's goals. Monitoring is an essential component of adaptive management in general, and of this CCP. Specific monitoring strategies have been integrated into the goals and objectives described in this CCP whenever possible.

Plan Amendment and Revision

CCPs are meant to evolve with each individual refuge unit, and the Improvement Act specifically requires that CCPs be formally revised and updated at least every 15 years. The formal revision process would follow the same steps as the CCP process (see Figure 3). In the meantime, the Service would review and update this CCP periodically (at least as often as every five years) based on the results of the adaptive management program. This CCP would also be informally reviewed by Refuge staff while preparing annual work plans and updating the Refuge database. It may also be reviewed during routine inspections or programmatic evaluations. Results of any or all of these reviews may indicate a need to modify the plan. The goals described in this CCP would not change until they are re-evaluated as part of the formal CCP revision process. The objectives and strategies, however, may be revised to address changing circumstances or to take advantage of increased knowledge of the resources on the Refuge. If changes are required, the level of public involvement and associated NEPA documentation would be determined by the Project Leader in accordance with Service policy.